1st Workshop on Gender-Inclusive Translation Technologies (GITT 2023)

Tampere, Finland
15 June 2023

Editors:

Eva Vanmassenhove
Beatrice Savoldi
Luisa Bentivogli
Joke Daems
Janica Hackenbuchner

ISBN: 978-1-7138-8996-0

Printed from e-media with permission by:

Curran Associates, Inc.
57 Morehouse Lane
Red Hook, NY 12571

Some format issues inherent in the e-media version may also appear in this print version.

Association for Computational Linguistics
209 N. Eighth Street
Stroudsburg, Pennsylvania 18360

Phone: 1-570-476-8006
Fax: 1-570-476-0860

acl@aclweb.org

Additional copies of this publication are available from:

Curran Associates, Inc.
57 Morehouse Lane
Red Hook, NY 12571 USA
Phone: 845-758-0400
Fax: 845-758-2633
Email: curran@proceedings.com
Web: www.proceedings.com

Gender-Inclusive Translation Technologies

Proceedings of the

1st Workshop on Gender-Inclusive Translation Technologies

15 June 2023

Edited by

Eva Vanmassenhove, Beatrice Savoldi, Luisa Bentivogli, Joke Daems, Janiça Hackenbuchner

DOI: 10.26116/w5b1-av529789464857177

Published by Open Press Tilburg University
Tilburg, the Netherlands
https://www.openpresstiu.org

Contents

Preface by the Workshop Organizers

This volume contains the proceedings of the First International Workshop on Gender-Inclusive Translation Technologies (GITT-2023)[1], hosted by the 24th Annual Conference of The European Association for Machine Translation (EAMT 2023)[2]. GITT is set out to focus on gender-inclusive language in translation and cross-lingual scenarios. The workshop brings together researchers from diverse areas, including industry partners, MT practitioners and language professionals. Also, GITT aims to encourage multidisciplinary research that develops and interrogates both solutions and challenges for addressing bias and promoting gender inclusivity in MT and translation tools.

The workshop welcomed three types of contributions: research papers, research communications, and extended abstracts. GITT-2023 received a total of 12 new submissions (10 research papers, 2 extended abstracts) and 1 research communication. Following the review process, 9 submissions were accepted (8 research papers and 1 abstract), resulting in an acceptance rate of 75% that highlights the quality of the submissions received. It is worth noting that the research communication did not undergo the review process as it had previously undergone peer-review at a top-tier conference. Of the accepted papers, 4 have been assigned to oral presentations, while the remaining 5, as well as the accepted abstract, have been assigned to the poster session. The research communication, which is not included in the proceedings, is also to be presented during the poster session in order to promote dissemination of research aligned with the scope of the workshop.

The accepted papers cover a diverse range of topics related to the analysis, measurement, and mitigation of gender bias in (Machine) Translation, as well as to the investigation of inclusive language. We are glad to attest to the interdisciplinary perspectives and methods represented in GITT submissions. The contributions range from technical papers proposing novel debiasing methods to position papers, user-centric surveys on the use of inclusive language, including also participatory research for community-informed fair MT.

In addition to the technical programme, we are honoured to have four invited speakers: Nizar Habash (New York University Abu Dhabi), with a keynote entitled "Computational Modeling of Gender in Arabic"; Danielle Saunders (RWS Language Weaver) with the keynote "Gender-Inclusive Machine Translation: Challenges and Needs"; Laura Hekanaho (Tampere University/University of Helsinki) and Anna Merikallio (University of Turku) who will give a

[1]https://sites.google.com/tilburguniversity.edu/gitt2023

[2]https://events.tuni.fi/eamt23/

joint keynote speech on "Gender in Finnish: Perspectives From Linguistics and Translation Studies".

Finally, the program includes a practical session and discussion based on the DeBiasByUs[3] initiative, which aims to raise public awareness about gender bias in MT and is creating a community-driven database of MT gender bias examples.

We sincerely thank all the people and institutions that contributed to the success of the workshop: the authors of the submitted papers for their interest in the topic; the Programme Committee members for their valuable feedback and insightful comments; the EAMT organizers for their support. Finally, we thank our sponsor, Ghent University, for its generous contribution.

We hope you enjoy reading the papers and are looking forward to a fruitful and enriching workshop!

June 2023,

Eva Vanmassenhove, Beatrice Savoldi, Luisa Bentivogli, Joke Daems & Janiça Hackenbuchner

[3] https://debiasbyus.ugent.be/

GITT 2023 Committees

Organising Committee & Workshop Chairs

Eva Vanmassenhove, Department Cognitive Science and Artificial Intelligence, School of Humanities and Digital Sciences, Tilburg University (TiU), Tilburg, The Netherlands
Beatrice Savoldi, Fondazione Bruno Kessler (FBK), Trento, Italy
Luisa Bentivogli, Fondazione Bruno Kessler (FBK), Trento, Italy
Joke Daems, Department Translation, Interpreting and Communication, Ghent University, Ghent 9000, Belgium
Janiça Hackenbuchner, Institute for Translation and Multilingual Communication, Cologne University of Applied Sciences, Germany

Programme Committee

Bashar Alhafni, New York University
Christine Basta, Alexandria University
Toms Bergmanis, University of Latvia
Dagmar Gromann, University of Vienna
Marcely Zanon Boito, NAVER LABS Europe
Danielle Saunders, RWS
Roberta Pederzoli, University of Bologna
Michal Měchura, Masaryk University
Declan Groves, Microsoft
Beatrice Spallaccia, University of Bologna
Manuel Lardelli, University of Graz
Johanna Monti, L'Orientale University of Naples
María Isabel Rivas Ginel, University of Burgundy/University of Valladolid

Workshop Program

Time	Activity
09:00 – 09:15	Start & Opening notes
09:15 – 10:30	**Keynote 1:** *Computational Modeling of Gender in Arabic* Nizar Habash
	Keynote 2: *Gender-Inclusive Machine Translation: Challenges and Needs* Danielle Saunders
10:30 – 11:00	Coffee break
11:00 – 12:30	**Oral Presentations**
	Reducing Gender Bias in NMT With FUDGE Tianshuai Lu, Noëmi Aepli and Annette Rios
	Gender Neutralization for an Inclusive Machine Translation: From Theoretical Foundations to Open Challenges Andrea Piergentili, Dennis Fucci, Beatrice Savoldi, Matteo Negri and Luisa Bentivogli
	Gender-Fair Language in Translation: A Case Study Angela Balducci Paolucci, Manuel Lardelli and Dagmar Gromann
	Gender-Inclusive Translation for a Gender-Inclusive Sport: Strategies and Translator Perceptions at the International Quadball Association Joke Daems
12:30 – 13:30	Lunch break
13:30 – 14:30	**Keynote 3:** *Gender in Finnish: Perspectives From Linguistics and Translation Studies* Laura Hekanaho and Anna Merikallio
14:30 – 15:00	**Poster Session**
	First the Worst: Finding Better Gender Translations During Beam Search Danielle Saunders, Rosie Sallis and Bill Byrne
	Gender Lost in Translation: How Bridging the Gap Between Languages Affects Gender Bias in Zero-Shot Multilingual Translation Lena Cabrera and Jan Niehues
	The User-Aware Arabic Gender Rewriter Bashar Alhafni, Ossama Obeid and Nizar Habash
	Participatory Research as a Path to Community-Informed, Gender-Fair Machine Translation Dagmar Gromann, Manuel Lardelli, Katta Spiel, Sabrina Burtscher, Lukas Daniel Klausner, Arthur Mettinger, Igor Miladinovic, Sigrid Schefer-Wenzl, Daniela Duh and Katharina Bühn
	Gender, Names and Other Mysteries: Towards the Ambiguous for Gender-Inclusive Translation Danielle Saunders and Katrina Olsen
	How Adaptive is Adaptive Machine Translation, Really? A Gender-Neutral Language Use Case Aida Kostikova, Joke Daems and Todor Lazarov
15:00 – 15:30	Coffee break
15:30 – 16:00	**Poster Session** (continued)
16:00 – 17:30	**Open Discussion** (guided by examples DeBiasByUs)

Research Papers

The User-Aware Arabic Gender Rewriter

Bashar Alhafni, Ossama Obeid, Nizar Habash
Computational Approaches to Modeling Language Lab
New York University Abu Dhabi
{alhafni,oobeid,nizar.habash}@nyu.edu

Abstract

We introduce the User-Aware Arabic Gender Rewriter, a user-centric web-based system for Arabic gender rewriting in contexts involving two users. The system takes either Arabic or English sentences as input, and provides users with the ability to specify their desired first and/or second person target genders. The system outputs gender rewritten alternatives of the Arabic sentences (provided directly or as translation outputs) to match the target users' gender preferences.

Bias Statement

Most NLP systems generate a single output for a specific input without taking their end users' grammatical gender preferences into consideration. Such systems typically result in output patterns that create representational harms by propagating biased stereotypes, such as associating certain professional activities or occupations with a particular gender. The system we present in this paper, allows the users to provide their desired gender preferences to provide them with user-aware unbiased outputs. We acknowledge that by limiting the choice of gender expressions to the grammatical gender choices in Arabic, we exclude other alternatives such as non-binary, gender-inclusive or no-gender expressions. We are aware of growing discussions around developing such alternatives in Arabic (UN, 2018; Ala'uldeen, 2022).

Figure 1: Google Translate's output for *"I am a doctor and you are a nurse"* in Arabic. Doctor is translated to the masculine form ('طبيب' *Tbyb*), whereas nurse is translated to the feminine form ('ممرضة' *mmrDħ*).

1 Introduction

Gender stereotypes, both negative and positive, are manifest in most of the world's languages (Maass and Arcuri, 1996; Menegatti and Rubini, 2017) and are further propagated and amplified by NLP systems (Sun et al., 2019; Blodgett et al., 2020) (see Figure 1). This is because NLP systems rely on human-created language corpora that mirror the societal biases and inequalities of the world we live in (Boyd and Crawford, 2012; Olteanu et al., 2019). For instance, Figure 2(a) presents part of a cooking recipe published on an Arabic popular cooking website targeting female readers,[1] whereas Figure 2(b) shows part of an article on career advice that is published on Harvard Business Review in Arabic targeting male readers.[2] However, even if overt gender biases are removed from datasets before using them to build NLP models,

[1] https://www.atyabtabkha.com/
[2] https://hbrarabic.com/

Figure 2: Examples of gender-specific text in the wild. Figure (a) is an example of text targeting female readers from a website about cooking recipes. The example is an introduction to a recipe for Baba Ghannouj. Figure (b) is an example of text targeting male readers from a website about career advice. The example is about an advice on how to find a new job. The underlined words are morphologically marked for the second person feminine in (a), and the second person masculine in (b).

this will not ultimately reduce the biases produced by systems that are designed to generate a single text output without taking their target users' gender preferences into consideration.

Some commercial NLP systems have solved this problem by generating more than one gender-specific output when the system encounters ambiguous scenarios. For instance, Google Translate generates both feminine and masculine translations when translating gender-neutral English sentences (e.g., *I am a doctor*) to a limited number of languages, such as Spanish (Kuczmarski, 2018; Johnson, 2020). However, this approach does not work well in multi-user contexts (first and second persons, with independent grammatical gender preferences), particularly when dealing with gender-marking morphologically rich languages. One example of this phenomenon is the Arabic machine translation of the sentence *I am a doctor and you are a nurse*. Figure 1 shows that Google Translate outputs the Arabic translation أنا طبيب وأنت ممرضة *ÂnA Tbyb wÂnt mmrDħ*[3] 'I am a [male] doctor and you are a [female] nurse', whereas a more suitable output would include all four possible Arabic translations of the input sentence.

One approach to mitigate the ambiguity is to provide the users with the ability to specify their desired target gender preferences so that NLP systems would generate personalized unbiased outputs. To this end, we build on the work of Alhafni et al. (2022b) where they formally introduced the task of gender rewriting and developed a user-centric gender rewriting model for Arabic.[4] We introduce the User-Aware Arabic Gender Rewriter, a user-centric web-based system for Arabic gender rewriting in contexts involving two users.[5] Our system takes either Arabic or English sentences as input, and provides users with the ability to specify their desired first and/or second person grammatical target genders. The system outputs gender rewritten alternatives of the Arabic input sentences (or their Arabic translations in case of English input) to match the target users' gender preferences. To the best of our knowledge, this is the first open-access web-based Arabic gender rewriting system.

Our goal behind creating an easy-to-use web-based multi-user Arabic gender rewriting tool is to enable users to rewrite any Arabic text based on their grammatical gender preferences that are consistent with their social identities. This reduces the gender bias that is caused by user-unaware NLP systems and increases the inclusiveness of Arabic NLP applications, leading to a better user experience. We envision a future in which websites such as those in Figure 2 could use automatic gender rewriting that fits the private preferences of their readers, or that is adjusted with simple website controls comparable to selecting different languages.

The rest of this paper is organized as follows. We discuss related work and Arabic linguistic facts in §2 and §3, respectively. We describe the design and implementation of the web-based Arabic gender rewriter in §4 and conclude in §5.

[3] Arabic HSB transliteration (Habash et al., 2007).

[4] https://github.com/CAMeL-Lab/gender-rewriting/

[5] http://gen-rewrite.camel-lab.com/

2 Related Work

Research has shown that NLP systems embed and amplify gender bias in a variety of core tasks such as machine translation (MT) (Rabinovich et al., 2017; Elaraby et al., 2018; Vanmassenhove et al., 2018; Escudé Font and Costa-jussà, 2019; Stanovsky et al., 2019; Costa-jussà and de Jorge, 2020; Gonen and Webster, 2020; Saunders and Byrne, 2020; Saunders et al., 2020; Stafanovičs et al., 2020; Savoldi et al., 2021; Ciora et al., 2021; Savoldi et al., 2022b; Savoldi et al., 2022a) and dialogue systems (Cercas Curry et al., 2020; Dinan et al., 2020; Liu et al., 2020a; Liu et al., 2020b; Sheng et al., 2021). Most existing solutions to mitigate gender bias in NLP systems either focus on debiasing pretrained representations used in downstream tasks (Bolukbasi et al., 2016; Zhao et al., 2018b; Manzini et al., 2019; Zhao et al., 2020) or on training systems on gender-balanced corpora (Lu et al., 2018; Rudinger et al., 2018; Zhao et al., 2018a; Hall Maudslay et al., 2019; Zmigrod et al., 2019).

More recently, text rewriting models were introduced to mitigate gender bias by either neutralizing the outputs of NLP systems or changing their grammatical genders to match provided users' gender preferences. Vanmassenhove et al. (2021) and Sun et al. (2021) presented rule-based and neural rewriting models to generate gender-neutral sentences in English. For morphologically rich languages and specifically Arabic, Habash et al. (2019) and Alhafni et al. (2020), introduced gender identification and rewriting models to rewrite first-person-singular Arabic sentences based on the target user gender requirements. The task of gender rewriting was formally introduced by Alhafni et al. (2022b) where they developed a new approach for Arabic gender rewriting in contexts involving two users (I and/or You) – first and second grammatical persons with independent grammatical gender preferences, and showed improvements over both Habash et al. (2019) and Alhafni et al. (2020) systems. The tool we introduce in this work uses the best gender rewriting model developed by Alhafni et al. (2022b).[4]

It is worth noting that our tool is similar to the recently introduced `Fairslator` (Měchura, 2022), a human-in-the-loop web-based tool for detecting and correcting gender bias in the output of MT systems translating from English to French, German, Czech, or Irish.[6] However, our work is different from theirs in the following ways:

- **Input**: our system takes either Arabic or English sentences as an input, whereas `Fairslator` only handles English sentences.
- **Models**: the Arabic gender rewriter relies internally on both rule-based and neural models as opposed to `Fairslator`'s rule-based gender reinflection system.
- **Evaluation**: the underlying gender rewriting model we use has been evaluated on Arabic gender rewriting and post-editing MT output, and it achieves state-of-the-art results, whereas `Fairslator` was not evaluated on any of the four languages it targets.
- **Visualization**: we focus on visualization by highlighting Arabic gender-marking words in both the input and the output to provide a better user-experience.

3 Arabic Linguistic Background

Arabic has a rich morphological system that inflects for gender, number, person, case, state, aspect, mood and voice, in addition to numerous attachable clitics (prepositions, particles, pronouns) (Habash, 2010). Arabic nouns, adjectives, and verbs inflect for gender: masculine (*M*) and feminine (*F*), and for number: singular (*S*), dual (*D*) and plural (*P*). Grammatical gender and number are commonly expressed using inflectional suffixes that represent some number and gender combination. Pronominal clitics also express gender and number combinations, e.g., طبيبتكم *Tbyb+km* 'your [masculine plural] doctor [feminine singular]. Gender and number participate in the morpho-syntactic agreement within specific constructions such as nouns and their adjectives and verbs and their subjects.

In practice, gender-specific words that are candidates for gender rewriting account for 10% of all words in all sentences and 17% of all words in gender-specific sentences. These statistics are calculated from the Arabic Parallel Gender Corpus (APGC) v2.1 (Alhafni et al., 2022a), which we use to train our models.

Figure 3: The Arabic Gender Rewriter interface showing gender rewritten alternatives of three input sentences in four modes: (a) Target speaker ♀ gender rewrites, (b) Target speaker ♀ and target listener ♀ and ♂ gender rewrites, (c) Target speaker ♀ and ♂ and target listener ♀ gender rewrites, and (d) Target speaker ♀ and ♂ and target listener ♀ and ♂ gender rewrites. Speaker gendered words are in blue and listener gendered words are in orange.

4 Design and Implementation

4.1 User Interface

Our gender rewriting interface is publicly available.[5] Figure 3(a) shows the basic structure of the interface. At the top, there is a text box to input either English or Arabic text. At each side of the text box, there are two selection buttons to indicate the desired target gender preferences for the speaker and the listener (♂ is for masculine and ♀ is for feminine). The user is able to select any possible combination of the desired target genders, including no target gender selection (i.e., requesting no rewriting).

Once the user clicks on the *Translate & Rewrite* button, all input English sentences will be passed to Google Translate's API to translate them into Arabic before generating their gender alternatives. When the gender rewriting process is done, additional text boxes will appear: the first text box will always contain the gender-identified Arabic inputs and the rest of the text boxes will contain the gender rewritten alternatives. Each gender marking word in the gender-identified input text box will be labeled as either masculine (♂) or feminine (♀). First-person (i.e., speaker) gendered words are colored in blue and second-person (i.e., listener) gendered words are colored in orange.

The number of the text boxes containing the gender rewritten alternatives is based on the selected target gender preferences. Each one of those boxes will have a label at its sides indicating a particular target gender combination based on the users' selections. For instance, Figure 3(a) has one text box containing first-person feminine gendered alternatives of the input sentences. We discuss the screenshots in Figure 3 in more details in §4.2.

Front-end The front-end was implemented using `Preact`[7] for view control and `Bulma`[8] for styling.

Back-end The back-end was implemented in Python using `Flask` to create a web API wrapper for the gender rewriting model.[9] We use the best performing gender rewriting model described in Alhafni et al. (2022b). The model was trained on the APGC v2.1 in addition to augmented data from the OpenSubtitles 2018 dataset (Lison and Tiedemann, 2016) and it consists of three components: gender identification, out-of-context word gender rewriting, and in-context ranking and selection.

The gender identification component identifies the word-level gender label for each word in the input sentence. It leverages a word-level BERT-based (Devlin et al., 2019) classifier that was built by fine-tuning CAMeLBERT MSA (Inoue et al., 2021). Once the gender labels have been identified for each word in the input and given the desired users target genders, out-of-context word gender rewriting is triggered based on the compatibility between the provided users' target genders and the predicted word-level gender labels. The gender rewriting component employs three word-level gender alternative generation models in a backoff cascade setup: 1) Corpus-based Rewriter: a bigram maximum likelihood estimation lookup model; 2) Morphological Rewriter: a morphological analyzer and generator provided by CAMeL Tools (Obeid et al., 2020); and 3) Neural Rewriter: a character-level sequence-to-sequence model with side constraints (Sennrich et al., 2016). Since the three implemented word-level gender rewriting models are out of context and given Arabic's morphological richness, this leads to producing multiple candidate gender alternative sentences. To select the best candidate output sentence, we rank all candidates in full sentential context based on their pseudo-log-likelihood scores (Salazar et al., 2020).

Results As we previously reported in Alhafni et al. (2022b), the results on the test set of APGC v2.1 show that the best gender rewriting model achieves an $\mathbf{M^2}$ $\mathbf{F_{0.5}}$ (Dahlmeier and Ng, 2012) score of **88.4** and an average of **1.2 BLEU** (Papineni et al., 2002) increase when automatically post-editing Google Translate's output.

4.2 Examples and Use Cases

Figure 3 presents the different outputs of the gender rewriting tool for three input sentences, one in English and two in Arabic. The three sentences come from the examples presented in Figure 1, Figure 2(a), and Figure 2(b), respectively.

In Figure 3(a), only the feminine target gender for the speaker is selected by the user. In this case, the system performs gender identification and then generates the first-person feminine gender alternative of the input sentences where all first-person masculine words are rewritten to feminine. Fig-

[6] `https://www.fairslator.com/`
[7] `https://preactjs.com/`
[8] `https://bulma.io/`
[9] `http://flask.pocoo.org/`

ure 3(b) shows an example where the feminine target gender for the speaker, and both the feminine and the masculine target genders for the listener are selected. In this case, the system outputs two gender rewritten alternatives for each input sentence, one for each selected target gender combination (i.e., speaker feminine – listener feminine, speaker feminine – listener masculine). Similarly, Figure 3(c) shows an example where both the feminine and the masculine target genders for the speaker, and the feminine target gender for the listener are selected. Lastly, Figure 3(d) is where all the target gender preferences are selected for both the speaker and the listener. In this case, the system generates all four possible gender rewritten alternatives for each input sentence.

5 Conclusion and Future Work

We introduced the User-Aware Arabic Gender Rewriter, a user-centric web-based system for Arabic gender rewriting in contexts involving two users. Our system takes either Arabic or English sentences as input, and provides users with the ability to specify their desired first and/or second persons target genders. The system outputs gender rewritten alternatives of the Arabic input sentences (or their Arabic translations in case of English input) to match the target users' gender preferences. Moreover, the system highlights Arabic gender-marking words in both the input and the output to provide a better user-experience.

In future work, we plan to continue improving our gender rewriting back-end by adding better gender rewriting models and enhancing inference efficiency, as well as expanding gender identification and rewriting to third person entities. We also plan to improve the interface by enabling users to provide feedback that can be collected and used to enhance the performance of gender rewriting. We will also improve the visualization we use to highlight Arabic gender marking words by examining the added value it provides to different end users, from language learners to native text editors.

References

Ala'uldeen, Rola. 2022. Gender and Arabic (in Arabic). Kohl Journal Vol 8. `https://kohljournal.press/node/346`.

Alhafni, Bashar, Nizar Habash, and Houda Bouamor. 2020. Gender-aware reinflection using linguistically enhanced neural models. In *Proceedings of the Second Workshop on Gender Bias in Natural Language Processing*, pages 139–150, Barcelona, Spain (Online), December. Association for Computational Linguistics.

Alhafni, Bashar, Nizar Habash, and Houda Bouamor. 2022a. The Arabic parallel gender corpus 2.0: Extensions and analyses. In *Proceedings of the Thirteenth Language Resources and Evaluation Conference*, pages 1870–1884, Marseille, France, June. European Language Resources Association.

Alhafni, Bashar, Nizar Habash, and Houda Bouamor. 2022b. User-centric gender rewriting. In *Proceedings of the 2022 Conference of the North American Chapter of the Association for Computational Linguistics: Human Language Technologies*, pages 618–631, Seattle, United States, July. Association for Computational Linguistics.

Blodgett, Su Lin, Solon Barocas, Hal Daumé III, and Hanna Wallach. 2020. Language (technology) is power: A critical survey of "bias" in NLP. In *Proceedings of the 58th Annual Meeting of the Association for Computational Linguistics*, pages 5454–5476, Online, July. Association for Computational Linguistics.

Bolukbasi, Tolga, Kai-Wei Chang, James Y Zou, Venkatesh Saligrama, and Adam T Kalai. 2016. Man is to computer programmer as woman is to homemaker? debiasing word embeddings. In Lee, D., M. Sugiyama, U. Luxburg, I. Guyon, and R. Garnett, editors, *Advances in Neural Information Processing Systems*, volume 29. Curran Associates, Inc.

Boyd, Danah and Kate Crawford. 2012. Critical questions for big data. *Information, Communication & Society*, 15(5):662–679.

Cercas Curry, Amanda, Judy Robertson, and Verena Rieser. 2020. Conversational assistants and gender stereotypes: Public perceptions and desiderata for voice personas. In *Proceedings of the Second Workshop on Gender Bias in Natural Language Processing*, pages 72–78, Barcelona, Spain (Online), December. Association for Computational Linguistics.

Ciora, Chloe, Nur Iren, and Malihe Alikhani. 2021. Examining covert gender bias: A case study in Turkish and English machine translation models. In *Proceedings of the 14th International Conference on Natural Language Generation*, pages 55–63, Aberdeen, Scotland, UK, August. Association for Computational Linguistics.

Costa-jussà, Marta R. and Adrià de Jorge. 2020. Fine-tuning neural machine translation on gender-balanced datasets. In *Proceedings of the Second Workshop on Gender Bias in Natural Language Processing*, pages 26–34, Barcelona, Spain (Online),

December. Association for Computational Linguistics.

Dahlmeier, Daniel and Hwee Tou Ng. 2012. Better evaluation for grammatical error correction. In *Proceedings of the 2012 Conference of the North American Chapter of the Association for Computational Linguistics: Human Language Technologies*, pages 568–572, Montréal, Canada, June.

Devlin, Jacob, Ming-Wei Chang, Kenton Lee, and Kristina Toutanova. 2019. BERT: Pre-training of deep bidirectional transformers for language understanding. In *Proceedings of the 2019 Conference of the North American Chapter of the Association for Computational Linguistics: Human Language Technologies, Volume 1 (Long and Short Papers)*, pages 4171–4186, Minneapolis, Minnesota, June. Association for Computational Linguistics.

Dinan, Emily, Angela Fan, Adina Williams, Jack Urbanek, Douwe Kiela, and Jason Weston. 2020. Queens are powerful too: Mitigating gender bias in dialogue generation. In *Proceedings of the 2020 Conference on Empirical Methods in Natural Language Processing (EMNLP)*, pages 8173–8188, Online, November. Association for Computational Linguistics.

Elaraby, Mostafa, Ahmed Y. Tawfik, Mahmoud Khaled, Hany Hassan, and Aly Osama. 2018. Gender aware spoken language translation applied to english-arabic. In *2018 2nd International Conference on Natural Language and Speech Processing (ICNLSP)*, pages 1–6.

Escudé Font, Joel and Marta R. Costa-jussà. 2019. Equalizing gender bias in neural machine translation with word embeddings techniques. In *Proceedings of the First Workshop on Gender Bias in Natural Language Processing*, pages 147–154, Florence, Italy, August. Association for Computational Linguistics.

Gonen, Hila and Kellie Webster. 2020. Automatically identifying gender issues in machine translation using perturbations. In *Findings of the Association for Computational Linguistics: EMNLP 2020*, pages 1991–1995, Online, November. Association for Computational Linguistics.

Habash, Nizar, Abdelhadi Soudi, and Tim Buckwalter. 2007. On Arabic Transliteration. In van den Bosch, A. and A. Soudi, editors, *Arabic Computational Morphology: Knowledge-based and Empirical Methods*, pages 15–22. Springer, Netherlands.

Habash, Nizar, Houda Bouamor, and Christine Chung. 2019. Automatic gender identification and reinflection in Arabic. In *Proceedings of the First Workshop on Gender Bias in Natural Language Processing*, pages 155–165, Florence, Italy, August.

Habash, Nizar Y. 2010. *Introduction to Arabic natural language processing*, volume 3. Morgan & Claypool Publishers.

Hall Maudslay, Rowan, Hila Gonen, Ryan Cotterell, and Simone Teufel. 2019. It's all in the name: Mitigating gender bias with name-based counterfactual data substitution. In *Proceedings of the 2019 Conference on Empirical Methods in Natural Language Processing and the 9th International Joint Conference on Natural Language Processing (EMNLP-IJCNLP)*, pages 5267–5275, Hong Kong, China, November.

Inoue, Go, Bashar Alhafni, Nurpeiis Baimukan, Houda Bouamor, and Nizar Habash. 2021. The interplay of variant, size, and task type in Arabic pre-trained language models. In *Proceedings of the Sixth Arabic Natural Language Processing Workshop*, pages 92–104, Kyiv, Ukraine (Virtual), April. Association for Computational Linguistics.

Johnson, Melvin. 2020. A scalable approach to reducing gender bias in google translate. Google AI Blog.

Kuczmarski, James. 2018. Reducing gender bias in google translate. Google Blog.

Lison, Pierre and Jörg Tiedemann. 2016. OpenSubtitles2016: Extracting large parallel corpora from movie and TV subtitles. In *Proceedings of the Tenth International Conference on Language Resources and Evaluation (LREC'16)*, pages 923–929, Portorož, Slovenia, May. European Language Resources Association (ELRA).

Liu, Haochen, Jamell Dacon, Wenqi Fan, Hui Liu, Zitao Liu, and Jiliang Tang. 2020a. Does gender matter? towards fairness in dialogue systems. In *Proceedings of the 28th International Conference on Computational Linguistics*, pages 4403–4416, Barcelona, Spain (Online), December. International Committee on Computational Linguistics.

Liu, Haochen, Wentao Wang, Yiqi Wang, Hui Liu, Zitao Liu, and Jiliang Tang. 2020b. Mitigating gender bias for neural dialogue generation with adversarial learning. In *Proceedings of the 2020 Conference on Empirical Methods in Natural Language Processing (EMNLP)*, pages 893–903, Online, November. Association for Computational Linguistics.

Lu, Kaiji, Piotr Mardziel, Fangjing Wu, Preetam Amancharla, and Anupam Datta. 2018. Gender bias in neural natural language processing.

Maass, Anne and Luciano Arcuri. 1996. Language and stereotyping. *Stereotypes and stereotyping*, pages 193–226.

Manzini, Thomas, Lim Yao Chong, Alan W Black, and Yulia Tsvetkov. 2019. Black is to criminal as caucasian is to police: Detecting and removing multiclass bias in word embeddings. In *Proceedings of the 2019 Conference of the North American Chapter of the Association for Computational Linguistics: Human Language Technologies, Volume 1 (Long and Short Papers)*, pages 615–621, Minneapolis, Minnesota, June. Association for Computational Linguistics.

Měchura, Michal. 2022. A taxonomy of bias-causing ambiguities in machine translation. In *Proceedings of the 4th Workshop on Gender Bias in Natural Language Processing (GeBNLP)*, pages 168–173, Seattle, Washington, July. Association for Computational Linguistics.

Menegatti, Michela and Monica Rubini. 2017. Gender bias and sexism in language. In *Oxford Research Encyclopedia of Communication*. Oxford University Press.

Obeid, Ossama, Nasser Zalmout, Salam Khalifa, Dima Taji, Mai Oudah, Bashar Alhafni, Go Inoue, Fadhl Eryani, Alexander Erdmann, and Nizar Habash. 2020. CAMeL tools: An open source python toolkit for Arabic natural language processing. In *Proceedings of The 12th Language Resources and Evaluation Conference*, pages 7022–7032, Marseille, France, May. European Language Resources Association.

Olteanu, Alexandra, Carlos Castillo, Fernando Diaz, and Emr Kıcıman. 2019. Social data: Biases, methodological pitfalls, and ethical boundaries. *Frontiers in Big Data*, 2.

Papineni, Kishore, Salim Roukos, Todd Ward, and Wei-Jing Zhu. 2002. BLEU: a Method for Automatic Evaluation of Machine Translation. In *Proceedings of the Conference of the Association for Computational Linguistics (ACL)*, pages 311–318, Philadelphia, Pennsylvania, USA.

Rabinovich, Ella, Raj Nath Patel, Shachar Mirkin, Lucia Specia, and Shuly Wintner. 2017. Personalized machine translation: Preserving original author traits. In *Proceedings of the 15th Conference of the European Chapter of the Association for Computational Linguistics: Volume 1, Long Papers*, pages 1074–1084, Valencia, Spain, April.

Rudinger, Rachel, Jason Naradowsky, Brian Leonard, and Benjamin Van Durme. 2018. Gender bias in coreference resolution. In *Proceedings of the 2018 Conference of the North American Chapter of the Association for Computational Linguistics: Human Language Technologies, Volume 2 (Short Papers)*, pages 8–14, New Orleans, Louisiana, June.

Salazar, Julian, Davis Liang, Toan Q. Nguyen, and Katrin Kirchhoff. 2020. Masked language model scoring. In *Proceedings of the 58th Annual Meeting of the Association for Computational Linguistics*, pages 2699–2712, Online, July. Association for Computational Linguistics.

Saunders, Danielle and Bill Byrne. 2020. Reducing gender bias in neural machine translation as a domain adaptation problem. In *Proceedings of the 58th Annual Meeting of the Association for Computational Linguistics*, pages 7724–7736, Online, July. Association for Computational Linguistics.

Saunders, Danielle, Rosie Sallis, and Bill Byrne. 2020. Neural machine translation doesn't translate gender coreference right unless you make it. In *Proceedings of the Second Workshop on Gender Bias in Natural Language Processing*, pages 35–43, Barcelona, Spain (Online), December. Association for Computational Linguistics.

Savoldi, Beatrice, Marco Gaido, Luisa Bentivogli, Matteo Negri, and Marco Turchi. 2021. Gender Bias in Machine Translation. *Transactions of the Association for Computational Linguistics*, 9:845–874, 08.

Savoldi, Beatrice, Marco Gaido, Luisa Bentivogli, Matteo Negri, and Marco Turchi. 2022a. On the dynamics of gender learning in speech translation. In *Proceedings of the 4th Workshop on Gender Bias in Natural Language Processing (GeBNLP)*, pages 94–111, Seattle, Washington, July. Association for Computational Linguistics.

Savoldi, Beatrice, Marco Gaido, Luisa Bentivogli, Matteo Negri, and Marco Turchi. 2022b. Under the morphosyntactic lens: A multifaceted evaluation of gender bias in speech translation. In *Proceedings of the 60th Annual Meeting of the Association for Computational Linguistics (Volume 1: Long Papers)*, pages 1807–1824, Dublin, Ireland, May. Association for Computational Linguistics.

Sennrich, Rico, Barry Haddow, and Alexandra Birch. 2016. Controlling politeness in neural machine translation via side constraints. In *Proceedings of the 2016 Conference of the North American Chapter of the Association for Computational Linguistics: Human Language Technologies*, pages 35–40, San Diego, California, June. Association for Computational Linguistics.

Sheng, Emily, Kai-Wei Chang, Prem Natarajan, and Nanyun Peng. 2021. "nice try, kiddo": Investigating ad hominems in dialogue responses. In *Proceedings of the 2021 Conference of the North American Chapter of the Association for Computational Linguistics: Human Language Technologies*, pages 750–767, Online, June. Association for Computational Linguistics.

Stafanovičs, Artūrs, Toms Bergmanis, and Mārcis Pinnis. 2020. Mitigating gender bias in machine translation with target gender annotations.

Stanovsky, Gabriel, Noah A. Smith, and Luke Zettlemoyer. 2019. Evaluating gender bias in machine translation. In *Proceedings of the 57th Annual Meeting of the Association for Computational Linguistics*, pages 1679–1684, Florence, Italy, July.

Sun, Tony, Andrew Gaut, Shirlyn Tang, Yuxin Huang, Mai ElSherief, Jieyu Zhao, Diba Mirza, Elizabeth Belding, Kai-Wei Chang, and William Yang Wang. 2019. Mitigating gender bias in natural language processing: Literature review. In *Proceedings of the 57th Annual Meeting of the Association for Computational Linguistics*, pages 1630–1640, Florence, Italy, July. Association for Computational Linguistics.

Sun, Tony, Kellie Webster, Apu Shah, William Yang Wang, and Melvin Johnson. 2021. They, them, theirs: Rewriting with gender-neutral english.

UN. 2018. Guidelines for gender-inclusive language in Arabic. `https://www.un.org/ar/gender-inclusive-language/guidelines.shtml`.

Vanmassenhove, Eva, Christian Hardmeier, and Andy Way. 2018. Getting gender right in neural machine translation. In *Proceedings of the 2018 Conference on Empirical Methods in Natural Language Processing*, pages 3003–3008, Brussels, Belgium, October-November.

Vanmassenhove, Eva, Chris Emmery, and Dimitar Shterionov. 2021. NeuTral Rewriter: A rule-based and neural approach to automatic rewriting into gender neutral alternatives. In *Proceedings of the 2021 Conference on Empirical Methods in Natural Language Processing*, pages 8940–8948, Online and Punta Cana, Dominican Republic, November. Association for Computational Linguistics.

Zhao, Jieyu, Tianlu Wang, Mark Yatskar, Vicente Ordonez, and Kai-Wei Chang. 2018a. Gender bias in coreference resolution: Evaluation and debiasing methods. In *Proceedings of the 2018 Conference of the North American Chapter of the Association for Computational Linguistics: Human Language Technologies, Volume 2 (Short Papers)*, pages 15–20, New Orleans, Louisiana, June.

Zhao, Jieyu, Yichao Zhou, Zeyu Li, Wei Wang, and Kai-Wei Chang. 2018b. Learning gender-neutral word embeddings. In *Proceedings of the 2018 Conference on Empirical Methods in Natural Language Processing*, pages 4847–4853, Brussels, Belgium, October-November.

Zhao, Jieyu, Subhabrata Mukherjee, Saghar Hosseini, Kai-Wei Chang, and Ahmed Hassan Awadallah. 2020. Gender bias in multilingual embeddings and cross-lingual transfer. In *Proceedings of the 58th Annual Meeting of the Association for Computational Linguistics*, pages 2896–2907, Online, July. Association for Computational Linguistics.

Zmigrod, Ran, Sabrina J. Mielke, Hanna Wallach, and Ryan Cotterell. 2019. Counterfactual data augmentation for mitigating gender stereotypes in languages with rich morphology. In *Proceedings of the 57th Annual Meeting of the Association for Computational Linguistics*, pages 1651–1661, Florence, Italy, July.

Gender-Fair Language in Translation: A Case Study

Angela Balducci Paolucci
University of Vienna, Austria
angelabalducci4@gmail.com

Manuel Lardelli
University of Graz, Austria
manuel.lardelli@uni-graz.at

Dagmar Gromann
University of Vienna, Austria
dagmar.gromann@gmail.com

Abstract

With an increasing visibility of non-binary individuals, a growing number of language-specific strategies to linguistically include all genders or neutralize any gender references can be observed. Due to this multiplicity of proposed strategies and gender-specific grammatical differences across languages, selecting the one option to translate gender-fair language is challenging for machines and humans alike. As a first step towards gender-fair translation, we conducted a survey with translators to compare four gender-fair translations from a notional gender language, English, to a grammatical gender language, German. Proposed translations were rated by means of best-worst scaling as well as regarding their readability and comprehensibility. Participants expressed a clear preference for strategies with gender-inclusive character, i.e., colon.

1 Introduction

Gender in language reflects on an extra-linguistic reality (Corbett, 1991) in the sense that it reflects gender associations and stereotypes of a society. To respect different gender identities, i.e., the sense of self and "who they are" (Barker and Iantaffi, 2019), it is vital to linguistically acknowledge their existence within and across languages. Machine translation (MT) is known to suffer from gender bias, which is problematic for many reasons. For instance, machine-translated online contents are consumed without people being aware that they are MT mediated (Martindale and Carpuat, 2018). In MT research, the idea to resort to gender-neutral language to avoid gender issues has been proposed (Piergentili et al., 2023). However, apart from information loss, this might not be the preferred gender-fair strategy by humans. To analyse human preferences, we propose a first survey[1] among language professionals of four distinct gender-fair translation strategies from English to German.

Translation studies has a long tradition of considering gender issues, such as in feminist (Von Flotow, 1997) and queer translation (Baer and Kaindl, 2017). However, gender beyond the binary has so far received little scholarly attention (e.g. Misiek (2020) and López (2022)). The same is true for the field of MT, where debiasing strategies focus on a binary conception of gender, with some important exceptions (Tomalin et al., 2021; Saunders and Byrne, 2020). Gender-fair language, which subsumes gender-inclusive and gender-neutral strategies, is particularly challenging in case of grammatical gender languages, i.e., several word classes require gender inflections.

In this case study, ten language professionals rated four gender-fair translations of online magazine articles in direct comparison and regarding their impact on readability and comprehensibility. The four German strategies consist of one gender-neutral neosystem, one gender-inclusive neosystem, a gender-inclusive colon with si:er, and the same colon with neopronoun xier. Since rating a translation is in general a highly subjective matter, the selected method is best-worst scaling, which allows participants to select and rate their subjectively most (best) and least (worst) preferred trans-

[1]The survey is made available on Zenodo: https://zenodo.org/record/7951054

Eva Vanmassenhove, Beatrive Savoldi, Luisa Bentivogli, Joke Daems & Janiça Hackenbuchner
Proceedings of the 1st Workshop on Gender-Inclusive Translation Technologes, p. 13–23
Tampere, Finland, June 2023.

lation. In a previous gender-fair MT workshop we conducted with translators, non-binary people, and MT experts (Burtscher et al., 2022), readability and comprehensibility of gender-fair language strategies were repeatedly named as important factors in the selection process. Thus, we decided to include a rating of these two dimensions in the present survey. Furthermore, participants were requested to motivate their choice in the form of a free text answer. While the perspective of non-binary individuals and MT experts would be equally interesting, we believe that preferences and considerations of language professionals as producers of (gender-fair) translations are of vital importance to the field of translation studies as well as machine translation. The results of this survey contribute to the discussion on which gender-fair language strategy is preferred in (machine) translating to German and which considerations are particularly important for language professionals.

2 Related Work

Since the focus of this article is on analyzing gender-fair translation strategies as a first step, this section focuses on work on gender-fair translation. In spite of the recent development of queer translation studies (Baer and Kaindl, 2017), research in the field of translation studies rarely addresses non-binary genders (Lardelli and Gromann, 2023). Most research focuses on media translation, e.g. subtitled and dubbed series, and news articles (López, 2022; Attig, 2022; Misiek, 2020; Šincek, 2020).

López (2019; 2022) and Attig (2022) analysed the dubbed and subtitled versions of the Netflix series *One Day at a Time* in Spanish and French. They found that the gender-fair language strategies used varied between the dubbed and subtitled versions as well as from European to Latin American Spanish. The non-binary character was correctly addressed with non-binary neopronoun *elle* in the European Spanish dubbed version only. In the other cases, they were misgendered with female forms and/or literal translations of English singular *they*. Similarly, in the French dubbed version, non-binary neopronoun *iell*e was used whereas in the subtitles the character was referred to with indefinite pronoun *on* (one/we).

In their analysis of English TV series translated to Polish, Misiek (2020) found a systematic omission of the non-binary characters' gender identity. This phenomenon could also be observed in Croatian movie translations and articles on Sam Smith's coming out as non-binary where the third person masculine plural pronoun was generally used (Šincek, 2020). Šincek (2020) represents also one of the few works to include interviews with people, i.e., non-binary individuals, on the topic.

Recent developments in gender-fair language strategies have been studied in psycholinguistics with a focus on binary genders. For instance, Lindqvist et al. (2019) conducted experiments in Swedish and English and tested different strategies to reduce male bias in language, i.e., (i) binary paired forms, (ii) gender-neutral words as well as (iii) gender-fair pronoun *hen* and English singular *they*. Participants read a description of a candidate for a job position and were asked to select photos of men or women corresponding to the said description. The results suggest that (i) and (iii) actively reduce male bias.

In German, empirical research concentrated on the cognitive processing of textual information. Braun et al. (2007), for example, tested the effect of male generics and two binary gender-fair language forms on memory performance and text intelligibility. No differences in memory performance across strategies were found between men and women. However, as concerns intelligibility, women indicated no preferences, while men indicated a preference for male generics.

To the best of our knowledge, this is the first study to consult language professionals regarding their preferences regarding gender-fair language strategies. Since language professionals play the important role of producing gender-fair translations, needed to fine-tune MT models, we believe that their perspective is interesting for translation studies and the field of machine translation.

3 Preliminaries

In order to establish the theoretical foundation of the present survey, an introduction to the interaction of gender with language and translation is provided, followed by a brief overview of gender-fair language strategies in English and German.

3.1 Gender and Language

The relation between gender and language is complex because the term has multiple meanings. In the field of gender studies, it is defined as a biopsychosocial construct (Barker and Iantaffi, 2019). It hence involves biological, e.g. hormonal, psychological, e.g. a person's sense of self, and social, e.g. normative and cultural expectations, factors. It is commonly used in reference to gender identity, i.e., a person's sense of their gender, and not the sex assigned at birth. In linguistics, the term is generally defined as "classes of nouns reflected in the behaviour of associated words" (Hockett, 1958, 231). In other words, associated word classes are inflected based on the grammatical gender of a specific noun.

Gender is realised differently in natural languages, which can be classified into (i) grammatical gender, (ii) notional gender, and (iii) genderless languages (Stahlberg et al., 2007; McConnell-Ginet, 2013). In (i), such as German and Italian, each noun has a gender (Corbett, 1991) and extensive gender marking is required. In (ii), such as English, third person singular pronouns, i.e., *he, she, it*, and specific nouns, e.g. *boy/girl*, are gender-specific. In (iii), such as Turkish, gender may be expressed, e.g. in kinship, but is not grammatically encoded in linguistic structures. Gender assignment in the case of human referents is based on the extra-linguistic reality of a society (Corbett, 1991) and reveals gender associations and stereotypes as well as connotations (Nissen, 2002; Jakobson, 1959).

3.2 Gender and Translation

Differences in linguistic structures and gender-specific connotations impact the translation process. In the first case, the translation from notional to grammatical gender languages can require choices that are not neutral (Nissen, 2002; Di Sabato and Perri, 2020). In several literary works, for instance *Written on the Body* (1993), a mysterious atmosphere is created by omitting gender markers. However, when translating to another language, this omission of gender might not be grammatically feasible, potentially forcing translators to assign a gender to characters (Di Sabato and Perri, 2020). This choice is often based on social gender, i.e., stereotypical associations to gender in a society (Nissen, 2002). In the second case, gender can be used to convey particular connotations through personifications and metaphors. This occurs, for example, in marketing texts and/or advertisement, where an animal, such as a male, fast tiger, is used to represent a car. Since the same animal can have different or no gender-specific connotations in other languages and cultures, translation choices that deliver the same source text message are required (Di Sabato and Perri, 2020).

3.3 Gender-Fair Language

Gender-fair language has a long tradition. Its development goes back to the 1960s, when differences in the linguistic treatment of men and women gained the attention of second-wave feminists (Kramer, 2016). With an increased visibility of non-binary people, new gender-fair language strategies have been accordingly proposed.

In English, singular *they* has become common to refer to people whose gender is unknown or irrelevant to the context of conversation as well as non-binary people (Apa Style, 2019). Furthermore, gender-neutral alternatives to gendered words, such as *chairperson* instead of *chairman*, are increasingly used (Weatherall, 2002). In German, a grammatical gender language that requires extensive gender marking, there are mainly four approaches:

- **gender-neutral rewording**: sentences are phrased in order to avoid gendered structures, e.g. person as gender-neutral word, indefinite pronouns, passive constructions and participial forms;

- **gender-inclusive characters**: typographic characters, such as gender star (*) or colon (:), are used to separate male forms from female endings and include all genders, e.g. *Leser*in* (reader). It is also possible to separate the stem from the noun ending as in *Lese*rin*, which should prevent binary thinking.

- **gender-neutral characters or endings**: for example *x* in *Lesx* (reader) are used to question the gender binary.

- **neosystems**:
  - gender-inclusive: a new gender is introduced in the language as in the case of the Sylvain system (De Sylvain and Balzer, 2008) with *Lesernin* (reader).
  - gender-neutral: the *ens* pronoun and suffix as in *Lesens* (reader) is introduced as gender-neutral form derived from M**ens**ch (human) (Hornscheidt and Sammla, 2021).

Furthermore, several neopronouns have been proposed. For instance, *xier* is the result of the combination of third person singular female *sie* and male *er* pronoun and has already been used in the translation of some English language TV series (Heger, 2020). Several more detailed overviews of gender-fair language in German are available (Hornscheidt, 2012; En et al., 2021; Hornscheidt and Sammla, 2021).

4 Method

In order to evaluate the perception, readability, and comprehensibility of gender-fair language strategies, two empirical methods targeted to measure subjective impressions were selected, i.e., Best-Worst Scaling (BWS) and the Likert scale. BWS (Louviere and Woodworth, 1990), a comparative annotation method, was used to select and evaluate the subjectively best and the worst translation strategy, whereas the Likert scale (Likert, 1932), a rating scale, was used to rate the readability and comprehensibility of the best and worst strategy chosen by the participants. Readability refers to whether a text written in a specific gender-fair language strategy is easy and enjoyable to read for the participants of this study subjectively. Comprehensibility refers to the ease to understand the message of a text written in a specific strategy for the participants of this study subjectively. The choice to combine these two methods is based on the desire to limit the granularity and inconsistencies that can occur when using solely a rating scale (Kiritchenko and Mohammad, 2017).

4.1 Data and Strategy Selection

Four English texts containing the use of singular *they* were selected from online articles to be translated using four different gender-fair language strategies. To be specific, the texts selected were interviews and reports on non-binary people in *Entertainment Weekly* (Text 1), *People* (Text 3) and on the website of the *Brown University* (Text 2) as well as a set of instructions on how to support a non-binary friend published on *Sociomix* (Text 4). Due to the fact that German is a grammatical gender language that associates gender with nouns in addition to pronouns, adjectives, and determiners, selected texts should allow to reflect this grammatical variety in the translation. For each original text, four gender-fair translations are provided in a set, which only differ in the utilized gender-fair language strategy. All translations were created manually and checked by three experts on gender-fair German. As strategies to be employed during the translation process, the choice fell on:

1. gender-neutral neosystem *ens*, because of its simple grammatical structure, where no declension and consequently easy use is expected;

2. gender-inclusive Sylvain neosystem, follows the grammatical rules of the German language, which is why it is expected to appear more natural;

3. colon after the word stem in combination with the pronoun *si:er*, because the colon is already widely known and used and with the two binary German pronouns combined should least impact readability and comprehensibility, and

4. colon after the word stem in combination with the *xier* pronoun, for the same reason of the colon and because the "x" explicitly emphasizes the inclusion of all genders, not only binary genders (Heger, 2013).

To exemplify the type of text and gender-fair translation strategies that were used in this study, we provide all four strategies for the sentence *Jim is a fierce pirate who journeys the seas seeking revenge on the people that killed their family.* of Text 1, an *Entertainment Weekly* interview with and article on Vico Ortiz who starred as non-binary pirate Jim in *Our Flag Means Death*:

1. Jim ist einens grimmig Piratens, dens durch die Meere reist, um sich an den Personen zu rächen, die ens Familie getötet haben.

2. Jim ist einin grimmigin Piratnin, din durch die Meere reist, um nimser an den Personen zu rächen, welche nimse Familie getötet haben.

3. Jim ist ei:ne Pira:tin, dier durch die Meere reist, um sich an den Personen zu rächen, welche siese Familie getötet haben.

4. Jim ist ei:ne Pira:tin, dier durch die Meere reist, um sich an den Personen zu rächen, welche xiese Familie getötet haben.

4.2 Participant Selection

For a principled selection of participating language professionals, a number of criteria had to be specified. First, their first language had to be German and they had to have a high command of English, i.e., C1 to C2 of the Common European Frame of Reference for Languages (CEFR), in order to be able to better identify which gender-fair strategy could be used as a translation for the English singular *they*. Second, participants were required to have completed or be about to complete a professional education in the field of translation. Finally, at least some practical translation experience beyond exercises during the education was required.

4.3 Survey Design

After introductory instructions and basic questions in a Google Forms survey, four translations corresponding to the four gender-fair strategies were presented side by side with the English original for each of the four source texts. For each pair of original and translations, participants were asked to select the best and the worst translation from the set and rate the former on a scale from +4 (very good) to 0 (neutral) and the latter from 0 (neutral) to -4 (very bad), a common scale and practice in BWS. Furthermore, participants were requested to rate the readability and comprehensibility of the best as well as worst translation selected on a Likert scale from 5 (very true) to 1 (not true). For the best strategy, the statements to be rated were that the best strategy does not impact the readability of the text and with the best gender-fair strategy the text is easy to understand. Thus, a rating of 5 means easy to read and highly comprehensible. For the worst strategy, the statements to be rated were that the worst strategy impacts the readability and makes the text hard to understand. Thus, a rating of 5 means hard to read and low comprehensibility. The general assumption was that the best strategy would have little impact on these two dimensions, while the worst is expected to achieve low ratings for both. Participants were also requested to optionally motivate their best/worst choices for each individual set of gender-fair translations as a free text answer. Furthermore, the demographic and general answers were analyzed to determine differences across participants and gather their prior experience with gender-fair language and translation as well as their opinion on the topic. The basic questions, thus, included participants' experience with and impressions on gender-fair language.

4.4 Analysis

The numeric BWS ratings are summed up by strategy across all four sets and all participants and divided by the number of times the strategy was rated to obtain the finally best and worst strategy on average in the survey. The same procedure was applied to the ratings on readability and comprehensibility. Finally, the free text answers and basic questions were analyzed and annotated for a topic-wise presentation of the results.

5 Results

After presenting participants' profiles, their preferences regarding the evaluated strategies, ratings for readability and comprehensibility, and overall comments on the topic are detailed.

5.1 Participant Profile

From the ten participants in the survey, nine identified as woman and one as man. In terms of age, 30% were between 18 and 25, 40% between 26 and 29, and 30% between 30 and 40. As required, all participants indicated to be professionally educated, have translation experience, and a high command of English (C1 or C2). All participants indicated to have prior knowledge of gender-fair language strategies, in particular neutral rewording and inclusive gender star and colon, and 90% indicated to be actively using gender-fair language in their daily lives. Another binary strategy that was indicated is to camel case plural endings with I to include men and women, e.g. *LeserInnen* instead of the female *Leserinnen* or the male *Leser*.

5.2 Ratings of Gender-Fair Translations

The detailed results of BWS ratings per participant, text, and gender-fair strategy are presented in Table 1. Each of the ten participants rated one translation per set as best and one as worst, resulting in a total of 40 positive/neutral and 40 negative/neutral ratings for four sets. Positive ratings are marked in green, negative ratings in red, and neutral ones in gray. The translation strategies in the columns correspond to the numbered list in Section 4.1, that is, S1 corresponds to the ens strategy, S2 the Sylvain system, S3 colon + si:er, and S4 colon + xier.

In Table 2, the counts of how often a strategy was selected as best or worst as well as the overall

Part.	Text 1 S1	Text 1 S2	Text 1 S3	Text 1 S4	Text 2 S1	Text 2 S2	Text 2 S3	Text 2 S4	Text 3 S1	Text 3 S2	Text 3 S3	Text 3 S4	Text 4 S1	Text 4 S2	Text 4 S3	Text 4 S4
P1		0		+3		0		+3		0		+3	+3	0		
P2		-4	+1			-2	+2			-3	+4			-1	+1	
P3		-3	+2			-3		+2	-2			+2		+3		-2
P4		-2	+3			-3	+3		-3		+4			-1	+4	
P5	-3		+2			-3		+3		-3	+3			-3		+4
P6		-4	0			-4	0		-4		0		-4		0	
P7	-4		0			0		+1	0			+2	0			+3
P8	+3	-2			+2	-1			+2	-2			+2	-2		
P9		-3	+3			-2	+3			-4	+3			-2	+3	
P10	-3			+2	-2			+2	-3			+2		-3		+2
Sum	-7	-18	+11	+5	0	-18	+8	+11	-10	-12	+14	+9	+1	-9	+8	+7

Table 1: Detailed BWS rating results per participant, strategy, and text

count and percentage it was selected are presented, alongside the sum, average and median BWS rating. The gender-fair translation strategy S4 obtained 18.75% of all ratings and achieved the best average rating of 2.13, followed by S3 with 25% of all ratings and on average 2.05 as can be seen from Table 2. While the Sylvain system obtained by far the most ratings, i.e., 36.25% of in total 80 ratings, from the numeric rating distribution and the color coding in Table 1 it becomes evident that it obtained mostly negative scores and the worst overall result with on average -1.97. Finally, S1 obtained 20% of all ratings and on average a final score of -1. Interestingly, S3 colon + si:er was never selected as worst strategy and did not obtain a single negative rating as can be seen from Table 1. Furthermore, it was most frequently selected as best strategy with 20 (50%) out of 40 positive rating counts. The overall best strategy S4 colon + xier was only selected once as worst strategy and obtained a negative rating by P3. Given that P3 breaks their previous pattern of rating S2 as worst, it might have been an accidental selection.

	S1	S2	S3	S4
Best C.	5	1	20	14
Worst C.	11	28	0	1
Total C.	16	29	20	15
Av. C. (%)	20.00	36.25	25.00	18.75
Sum R.	-16	-57	41	32
Av. R.	-1.00	-1.97	2.05	**2.13**
Median R.	-2.00	-3.00	3.00	2.00

Table 2: Summary of BWS rating results (C = Count; R = Rating; Av = Average)

While the decision that the S2 Sylvain system is the worst strategy was quite unanimous, some participants revealed individual preferences as can be seen in Table 1. Participant P8 showed a strong preference for the S1 ens strategy for all texts, while overall S1 obtained more negative than positive or neutral ratings. In terms of intra-annotator consistency, participants P2, P8, and P9 are completely consistent in their selection of strategies across texts. Other participants, especially P3, P5, and P7 changed their preferred strategies depending on the text, in particular with Text 3 and Text 4. This change could be attributed to the fact that the first two texts are equivalent in type since both are interviews, while Text 3 is a report on Demi Lovato and Text 4 represents a set of instructions of how to support a non-binary friend. Thus, there is considerable inter-annotator variation, however, overall the consensus is that colon with xier is the best and the Sylvain system is the worst gender-fair translation strategy for this group of participants.

5.3 Readability and Comprehensibility

Since in previous interactions with the target group of this study readability and comprehensibility were named as important factors for the choice of gender-fair language, participants were asked to rate both dimensions for the selected best and worst strategy. In Table 3 the average score for the best and worst strategy for both dimensions is provided, where for the best strategy 5 means high readability and comprehensibility and 1 means low readability and comprehensibility. For the worst strategy, participants were asked whether they agree that the strategy negatively influences readability and comprehensibility, which means

Best	S1	S2	S3	S4
Readability	3.40	3.00	2.95	3.07
Comprehensibility	3.60	3.00	3.00	3.21
Worst	**S1**	**S2**	**S3**	**S4**
Readability	4.55	3.86	0.00	4.00
Comprehensibility	4.55	3.50	0.00	4.00

Table 3: Average score on readability and comprehensibility

that full agreement (5) indicates low readability and comprehensibility, while 1 indicates a high rating for both dimensions.

As is to be expected, the strategies that were selected as worst were also rated as low in readability and comprehensibility, where S1 was on average indicated as the strategy with the highest impact on both dimensions. Table 3 confirms the fact that S3 was never selected as worst strategy by any participant. Ratings for the best strategy are more surprising, since even though participants considered a strategy the comparatively best from the set, they still indicated an impact on how easy to read and comprehend the gender-fair text is. On average, the ratings are rather neutral around 3, with only slightly worse ratings for the ens strategy (S1).

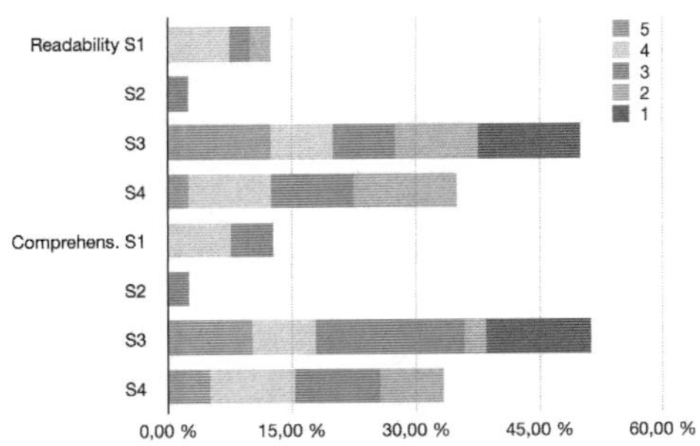

Figure 1: Detailed Scores of Best Strategy

To provide a closer look at the ratings of the best strategy, a detailed overview of scores is depicted in Fig. 1. S3 colon + si:er was selected most frequently as best strategy, which means it obtained most ratings for readability and comprehensibility. From the overall 20 ratings for S3 as best strategy, 9 (45%) ratings were very low with 1 or 2. Comprehensibility seems to be less of an issue, since only 6 (30%) ratings were below 3. In fact, as can be seen from Fig. 1, S3 is the only strategy to ever obtain a rating as low as 1 for both dimensions. However, it should be kept in mind here that with a small sample, single participants have an impact. Participant P6 consequently rated both dimensions as very low for a strategy across all texts, making up 4 of the 20 ratings for S3 as best strategy and of its readability and comprehensibility. This is in line with the overall evaluation of BWS, where P6 would never assign a higher score than 0 to any strategy (see Table 1). For S1 the results mostly rely on P8, who consistently selected it as the best strategy and considered both dimensions as high. P1 selected S1 ens only once as best strategy and provided a low rating for readability. An increase in scores from Text 1 to later texts could be explained by an increase in familiarity with the strategy, as commented by one participant. Overall readability seems to be a bigger issue than comprehensibility.

5.4 Participant Comments

Free text comments on the individual texts as well as on the survey in general reflected the overall negative attitude of participants towards the S2 Sylvain system. Participants remarked that texts written with this gender-fair language strategy would not be intelligible without the English original and especially the meaning of pronouns is hard to understand even in context, requiring an unnecessary cognitive effort. This comment reinforced our research design choice to provide the English original alongside the translations. One participant considered simply omitting possessive pronouns with this strategy as the best option. Other comments included that it generates texts that are perceived as grammatically incorrect, unnatural, and unnecessarily complicated, inhibiting the natural flow of the text.

In reference to S1, the ens system, participants mainly remarked on a detrimental effect on comprehensibility in their comments, which is in line with the fact that S1 obtained the worst overall ratings on comprehensibility in the survey. P5 remarked that they had to read the text several times in order to grasp its meaning and for P4 the text with this strategy seemed as if written in Dutch, distracting them from understanding it. P8, the only and most fervent advocate for S1, stated that to them it is the simplest strategy that is easy to use, both in written and spoken communication. Furthermore, to P8 ens imitates the English *they*, making it the ideal strategy for gender-fair translation from English. On the other hand, P8 remarks that the lack of noun declensions with this strategy might not be ideal.

In reference to the two best rated strategies with colon after the word stem, participants remarked that pronouns at times still seem unfamiliar, especially possessive pronouns, e.g. *sieser*, might at first be confused with demonstrative articles, e.g. *dieser*. Nevertheless, participants noted that it is comparatively easy to familiarize themselves with this strategy, which has little negative impact on the readability of the text.

One interesting change of comments from the first to the last set of English original and translations could be observed with participant P7, who on Text 1 commented that all of the proposed strategies have an entirely negative impact on readability. For Text 2, the remark changes to colon with xier might not be entirely unreadable, which progresses to relatively easy to read in Text 4. This change of heart is reflected in P7's ratings of the dimension readability, which progresses from 1 for the best strategy in Text 1 to 3 for the best strategy in Text 3 and 4. Comprehensibility never obtains a higher rating than 2. P7 finally concludes that the colon is less distracting also for pronouns than xier and its corresponding declensions.

As an overall evaluation of the entire survey, P7 provides an explicitly negative attitude towards the topic as such and an explicitly low opinion of gender-fair language in general, indicating to not use any such strategy privately and expressing the belief that a general public can hardly be expected to utilize such "creations". This overall belief is shared by P6, who provides low ratings for the best strategy as well as its readability and comprehensibility and at the end of the survey remarks that, while the topic is interesting, none of the proposed strategies find their liking and will hardly be used in everyday communication.

All participants but one considered the topic of gender-fair language strategies in translation interesting and important. Beyond the proposed strategies, the repetition of names instead of pronouns or rewording of nouns in the translation were indicated. One important aspect that was mentioned is the familiarity with and prior knowledge of the topic. Participants indicated that readability and comprehensibility improved from Text 1 to Text 4, highlighting how fast they were able to get more accustomed to these strategies. This factor of being accustomed and familiar with the individual strategies might in the end also change the overall evaluation, which for now leans towards S3 and S4 as the strategies closest to the current German language use.

6 Discussion

One initial assumption of this survey was that the gender-inclusive Sylvain system might be preferred on the basis that it follows the grammatical rules of German and thus, might seem more natural than other strategies. However, this strategy was overwhelmingly rated as the worst in the set, appearing unnatural, erroneous, confusing, and overly complex. Its ratings on readability and comprehensibility reflect these comments. The overall correspondence between BWS ratings and Likert scores indicates a tight link between personal preferences for gender-fair translation strategies and their subjective readability and comprehensibility, emphasizing the importance of the two dimensions chosen for this study. However, in future research these dimensions should take the specific needs of people with physical and/or cognitive disabilities into consideration, e.g. by conducting a survey with a more diverse group of participants.

The gender-neutral ens system is comparatively easy to use from a grammatical point of view, since it requires no declensions. However, this grammatical simplicity considerably alters the language with a detrimental effect on readability and comprehensibility, as shown by the overall ratings and participants' comments. Even its only advocate in the survey doubted the general applicability of a language system without declensions in German.

In the set of proposed strategies the colon after the word stem emerged as the clear winner, with a slight preference for its use with the neopronoun xier over introducing another colon in the pronouns as in si:er. Since these two strategies, S3 and S4, are the ones closest to the current language use, it can be assumed that familiarity with strategies plays a role in the selection of preferences, which was reflected in a participants' comment. Thus, it would be interesting to evaluate whether a thorough introduction including exercises to the other strategies would alter the final selection of preferred strategies. In fact, in a previously conducted workshop (Burtscher et al., 2022), participants obtained such a thorough introduction and then in exercises opted for the ens strategy (S1). One participant in this case study even remarked on the fact that familiarity, readability, and comprehensibility already increased from the first to the last text, where each of which was very short. This indicates that familiarizing participants with different strategies might be feasible in a large-scale survey or experimental setting and would be an interesting alternation for future studies on gender-fair translation.

Due to the multiplicity of proposed gender-fair language strategies in German, we opted for a small selection in this survey in order not to overwhelm participants. This selection was driven by the intention to compare gender-neutral and gender-inclusive strategies. However, for the former we only included one neosystem, where other strategies, such as rewording, are available. For the latter category, three strategies were included, where even for the best strategy a change in typographical character might already impact the responses, i.e., underscore or star instead of colon as well as placement of the character. The colon after the word stem was explicitly chosen to reduce the emphasis on male/female endings.

Since we only included one gender-neutral option, a subselection of gender-inclusive strategies and a sample limited in size, no conclusions on the preference of either category can be drawn, for which future studies with a different setup are foreseen. However, the importance to be equipped with gender-fair translation strategy that finds acceptance by the general public was emphasized. Thereby, common translation problems, such as involuntary or accidental misgendering in the translation, could be mitigated or solved. For instance, if the source text is rather vague on the gender of a character/person in a notional gender language, some gender-fair translation strategies enable equal vagueness in a grammatical gender language. While the best strategy ultimately depends on the context not only in the textual sense but also in the sense of the translation assignment, target group, purpose, etc., some strategies might be easier to use, comprehend, and read than others and might impact the transfer from the source to the target text differently.

In terms of implications for translation technologies and in particular machine translation, we believe that this survey reveals how complex and language-specific the topic of gender-fair language and translation truly is. While overall preferred strategies could be identified, individual participants showed different preferences, e.g. one participant clearly preferred the ens strategy. Thus, machine translation might need to be able to accommodate different gender-fair language strategies depending on the language, context, purpose, and target audience of a translation. These preferences or requirements might also change with the domain of texts, where in this case study the degree of domain-specificity of media texts is rather low. In this case study, the task was also to select from a set of existing translations. It would be interesting to evaluate the performance and preferences of professional translators when asked to perform gender-fair post-editing of machine translated texts.

7 Conclusion

In order to socially and linguistically include different gender identities, a multiplicity of gender-fair language strategies, in particular for grammatical gender languages, has been proposed. The transfer of gender-fair strategies across structurally different languages is challenging for machines and humans. Thus, it is interesting to evaluate the position and preferences of language professionals on the topic of gender-fair translation from a notional to a grammatical gender language. In the presented survey results based on best-worst scaling, ten language professionals revealed a preference for the gender-inclusive strategy of colon after the word stem in combination with the neopronoun xier over the gender-inclusive Sylvian and gender-neutral ens neosytem. The alternative of colon with si:er was rated only slightly lower than with xier, where participants commented on a preference for pronouns without typographical character that they considered more natural. For both strategies with colon the overall rating on the dimensions of readability and comprehensibility was neutral to positive, whereas ens was considered to negatively impact both dimensions the most. A correspondence between the expression of preferences and the ratings of readability and comprehensibility as well as explicit references to these two dimensions in free text comments confirmed their importance within the context of gender-fair translation strategies.

In the present study, a preference for a gender-inclusive strategy could be observed, however, with a limited selection of strategies and a small number of respondents. To obtain a general preference regarding gender-neutral or gender-inclusive strategies, a large-scale study with a stronger variety of gender-fair language strategies across languages and a larger, potentially more diverse target group would be required. The results indicate that preferences might also vary depending on the participants' degree of familiarity with individual strategies, which is a factor worth investigating in future endeavors. Finally, the impact of the level of domain specificity and text type would be interesting factors. Nevertheless, with this first study on gender-fair translation among language professionals we hope to have provided a methodological contribution as well as first results on gender-fair translation strategies from the perspective of language professionals, a method that can easily be transferred to future studies and even evaluating machine translation results.

References

Apa Style. 2019. Singular "they".

Attig, Remy. 2022. A call for community-informed translation: Respecting queer self-determination across linguistic lines. *Translation and Interpreting Studies*.

Baer, Brian James and Klaus Kaindl. 2017. Introduction: Queer (ing) translation. In Baer, Brian James and Klaus Kaindl, editors, *Queering Translation, Translating the Queer*, pages 1–10. Routledge.

Barker, Meg John and Alex Iantaffi. 2019. *Life isn't Binary*. London, UK: Jessica Kingsley Publishers.

Braun, Friederike, Susanne Oelkers, Karin Rogalski, Janine Bosak, and Sabine Sczesny. 2007. "aus gründen der verständlichkeit...": Der einfluss generisch maskuliner und alternativer personenbezeichnungen auf die kognitive verarbeitung von texten. *Psychologische Rundschau*, 58(3):183–189.

Burtscher, Sabrina, Katta Spiel, Daniel Lukas Klausner, Manuel Lardelli, and Dagmar Gromann. 2022. "es geht um respekt, nicht um technologie": Erkenntnisse aus einem interessensgruppen-übergreifenden workshop zu genderfairer sprache und sprachtechnologie. In *Mensch und Computer 2022*. ACM.

Corbett, Greville G. 1991. *Gender*. Cambridge University Press.

De Sylvain, Cabala and Carsten Balzer. 2008. Die sylvain-konventionen–versuch einer "geschlechtergerechten" grammatik-transformation der deutschen sprache. *Liminalis*, 2:40–53.

Di Sabato, Bruna and Antonio Perri. 2020. Grammatical gender and translation: A cross-linguistic overview. In von Flotow, Luise and Kamal Hala, editors, *The Routledge Handbook of Translation, Feminism and Gender*, pages 363–373. Routledge.

En, Boka, Tobias Humer, Marija Petričević, Tinou Ponzer, Claudia Rauch, and Katta Spiel. 2021. Geschlechtersensible Sprache – Dialog auf Augenhöhe.

Heger, Illi Anna. 2013. Version 3.2 : Xier pronomen ohne geschlecht.

Heger, Illi Anna. 2020. Version 3.3 : Xier pronomen ohne geschlecht.

Hockett, Charles F. 1958. *A Course in Modern Linguistics*. New York: Macmillan.

Hornscheidt, Lann and Ja'n Sammla. 2021. *Wie schreibe ich divers? Wie spreche ich gendergerecht?: Ein Praxis-Handbuch zu Gender und Sprache*. Insel Hiddensee: w_orten & meer.

Hornscheidt, Lann. 2012. *feministische w_orte: ein lern-, denk- und handlungsbuch zu sprache und diskriminierung, gender studies und feministischer linguistik*. Frankfurt: Brandes & Apsel.

Jakobson, Roman. 1959. On linguistic aspects of translation. In Brower, Reuben Arthur, editor, *On Translation*, pages 232–239. Cambridge.

Kiritchenko, Svetlana and Saif M Mohammad. 2017. Best-worst scaling more reliable than rating scales: A case study on sentiment intensity annotation. *arXiv preprint arXiv:1712.01765*.

Kramer, Elise. 2016. Feminist linguistics and linguistic feminisms. In Lewin, Ellen and Leni M. Silverstein, editors, *Mapping Feminist Anthropology in the Twenty-first Century*, pages 65–83. Rutgers University Press.

Lardelli, Manuel and Dagmar Gromann. 2023. Gender-fair (machine) translation. In *Proceedings of the New Trends in Translation and Technology Conference - NeTTT 2022*, pages 166–177.

Likert, Rensis. 1932. A technique for the measurement of attitudes. *Archives of psychology*.

Lindqvist, Anna, Emma Aurora Renström, and Marie Gustafsson Sendén. 2019. Reducing a male bias in language? establishing the efficiency of three different gender-fair language strategies. *Sex Roles*, 81:109–117.

López, Ártemis. 2019. Tú, yo, elle y el lenguaje no binario. *La Linterna del Traductor*, 19.

López, Ártemis. 2022. Trans (de) letion: Audiovisual translations of gender identities for mainstream audiences. *Journal of Language and Sexuality*, 11(2):217–239.

Louviere, Jordan J and George G Woodworth. 1990. Best worst scaling: A model for largest difference judgments [working paper]. *Faculty of Business*.

Martindale, Marianna J. and Marine Carpuat. 2018. Fluency over adequacy: A pilot study in measuring user trust in imperfect MT. *CoRR*, abs/1802.06041.

McConnell-Ginet, Sally. 2013. Gender and its relation to sex: The myth of 'natural'gender. In Corbett, Greville G, editor, *The Expression of Gender*, pages 3–38. De Gruyter Mouton.

Misiek, Szymon. 2020. Misgendered in Translation?: Genderqueerness in Polish Translations of English-language Television Series. *Anglica. An International Journal of English Studies*, 29(2):165–185.

Nissen, Uwe Kjær. 2002. Aspects of translating gender. *Linguistik online*, 11(2):25–37.

Piergentili, Andrea, Dennis Fucci, Beatrice Savoldi, Luisa Bentivogli, and Matteo Negri. 2023. From inclusive language to gender-neutral machine translation. *CoRR*, abs/2301.10075.

Saunders, Danielle and Bill Byrne. 2020. Reducing gender bias in neural machine translation as a domain adaptation problem. *arXiv preprint arXiv:2004.04498*.

Stahlberg, Dagmar, Friederike Braun, Lisa Irmen, and Sabine Sczesny. 2007. Representation of the sexes in language. *Social Communication*, pages 163–187.

Tomalin, Marcus, Bill Byrne, Shauna Concannon, Danielle Saunders, and Stefanie Ullmann. 2021. The practical ethics of bias reduction in machine translation: Why domain adaptation is better than data debiasing. *Ethics and Information Technology*.

Von Flotow, Luise. 1997. *Translation and Gender: Translating in The 'Era of Feminism'*. Routledge.

Weatherall, Ann. 2002. *Gender, language and discourse*. Hove: Routledge.

Winterson, Jeanette. 1993. *Written on the Body*. Random House.

Šincek, Marijana. 2020. *On, ona, ono*: Translating Gender Neutral Pronouns into Croatian. *Journal of the International Symposium of Students of English, Croatian and Italian Studies*, pages 92–112.

Gender Lost In Translation: How Bridging The Gap Between Languages Affects Gender Bias in Zero-Shot Multilingual Translation

Lena Cabrera[1], Jan Niehues[2]
[1]Department of Advanced Computing Sciences, Maastricht University, The Netherlands
[2]Institute for Anthropomatics and Robotics, Karlsruhe Institute of Technology, Germany
l.cabreraperez@student.maastrichtuniversity.nl,
jan.niehues@kit.edu

Abstract

Neural machine translation (NMT) models often suffer from gender biases that harm users and society at large. In this work, we explore how bridging the gap between languages for which parallel data is not available affects gender bias in multilingual NMT, specifically for zero-shot directions. We evaluate translation between grammatical gender languages which requires preserving the inherent gender information from the source in the target language. We study the effect of encouraging language-agnostic hidden representations on models' ability to preserve gender and compare pivot-based and zero-shot translation regarding the influence of the bridge language (participating in all language pairs during training) on gender preservation. We find that language-agnostic representations mitigate zero-shot models' masculine bias, and with increased levels of gender inflection in the bridge language, pivoting surpasses zero-shot translation regarding fairer gender preservation for speaker-related gender agreement.

1 Introduction

With the rapid proliferation of intelligent systems, machine learning models reflecting patterns of discriminatory behavior found in the training data is a growing concern of practitioners and academics. Neural machine translation (NMT) models have proven notoriously gender-biased, often resulting in harmful gender stereotyping or an under-representation of the feminine gender in their outputs. In recent years, several approaches to debias NMT have been proposed, including debiasing the data before model training, the models during training, or post-processing their outputs. However, to the best of the authors' knowledge, it has yet to be explored how the phenomenon of not observing enough data, if any, to model language accurately affects gender discrimination in multilingual NMT (MNMT).

To support translation between language pairs never seen during training (i.e., zero-shot directions), two widely-used approaches leverage the language resources (i.e., parallel data) available during training: *Pivot-based* translation uses an intermediate pivot/bridge language (as in source→pivot→target), whereas *zero-shot* translation learns to bridge the gap between unseen language pairs using cross-lingual transfer learning.[1]

In this work, we analyze gender bias in MNMT in the context of *gender preservation*, where gender information conveyed by the source language sentence needs to be preserved in the target language translation; in our experimental setting, source and target languages are grammatical gender languages that use a noun class system conforming with the *gender binary*, i.e., the classification of gender into the opposite forms of feminine and masculine, considered indicative of a person's biological sex.[2] We examine translations

[1]We use "zero-shot *directions*" to refer to language pairs unseen during training, whereas "zero-shot *translation*" is NMT capable of zero-shot inference, relying on a model's generalizability to conditions unseen during training.

[2]While gender, as opposed to biological sex, is viewed as a non-binary spectrum, many languages have not (yet) evolved beyond the male-female gender binary regarding linguistic gender when it ideally should correlate with biosocial gender.

in terms of differences in gender preservation between both genders, which, if found, are evidence of gender-biased machine translation (MT). More precisely, we focus on the impact that *bridging the gap between unseen language pairs* has on the MT models' ability to preserve the feminine and masculine gender, unambiguously indicated by the source sentence, equally well in their outputs. Our research questions are:

RQ1 How do zero-shot and pivot-based translation compare regarding gender-biased outputs for zero-shot directions?

RQ2 Does the bridge language affect the gender biases perpetuated by zero-shot and pivot-based translations?

RQ3 Do translation quality improvements of zero-shot models reduce their gender biases?

The remainder of this paper is structured as follows. Section 2 introduces the task of gender preservation in translation with relevant terminology and reviews related work on gender bias in NMT. Section 3 describes our experimental design, tailored toward investigating cause-and-effect relationships of gender bias in MNMT. Section 4 presents the data used and the evaluative procedure followed in our experiments. Section 5 presents the experimental setup and results, and Section 6 concludes with our summarized findings, limitations, and future research directions.

2 Terminology & Related Work

In a large-scale analysis of the plethora of existing research addressing gender bias in NMT, Savoldi et al. (2021) categorize them based on two conceptualizations of the problem: research works focusing on the weight of prejudice and stereotypes in NMT, and studies assessing whether gender is preserved in translation. In this paper, we analyze gender bias in MNMT in the context of gender preservation, where for translation into a gender-sensitive target language, the gender information conveyed by the source language needs to be retained in the target language translation.

Gender in Lingustics: In our gender bias evaluation we consider *referential gender*, which, according to Cao and Daumé III (2021), only exists when an entity (i.e., a human) is mentioned and their gender (or sex) is realized linguistically. Moreover, we focus on the translation between languages using *grammatical gender*, a way of classifying nouns, assigning them gender categories (e.g., masculine, feminine, neuter, etc.) that may be independent of the real-world biosocial genders associated with referents; however, there is a tendency for languages to correlate grammatical gender with the gender of a referent, especially if human (Corbett, 1991; Ackerman, 2019).

For example, talking about a specific doctor (e.g., "the doctor loves her_F job"), the word choice of the female anaphoric pronoun is not determined by grammatical gender but only by referential gender. The same sentence translated into German ("die_F $Ärztin_F$ liebt $ihren_F$ Job_M.") requires the article ("die" = the) and pronoun ("ihren" = her) to agree with the feminine grammatical gender category the noun is assigned ("Ärztin" = female doctor).[3] On the other hand, the sentence "the doctor helps the nurse" without any further context information does not indicate the gender of either of the two mentioned entities; for the German translation, the gender of both the doctor ("$Arzt_M$"/"$Ärztin_F$") and the nurse ("$Krankenpfleger_M$"/"$Krankenschwester_F$") needs to be considered for the correct syntactic build-up of the sentence. For details on the many differences in the manifestation of gender in languages, we refer the interested reader to related works such as that of Cao and Daumé III (2021).

Gender Preservation: Translation into a gender-sensitive language, e.g., a grammatical gender language, involves gender agreement between nominal properties—e.g. grammatical and referential gender of a (pro)noun—and a determiner, adjective, verb, etc., depending on the target language agreement rules. Whenever the source language is (largely) genderless, i.e., the gender of the noun is unspecified, and context information is unavailable, gender preservation is a non-trivial task for machines and humans alike.

In recent years, several approaches have been proposed to address the challenge of gender preservation. Vanmassenhove et al. (2018) leverage additional gender information by prepending a gender tag to each source sentence, both at training and inference time, to improve the generation of speakers' referential markings. Avoiding the need

[3] Note, in German, the abstract noun "Job" is assigned the masculine grammatical gender category, while in English, "job" has no grammatical gender.

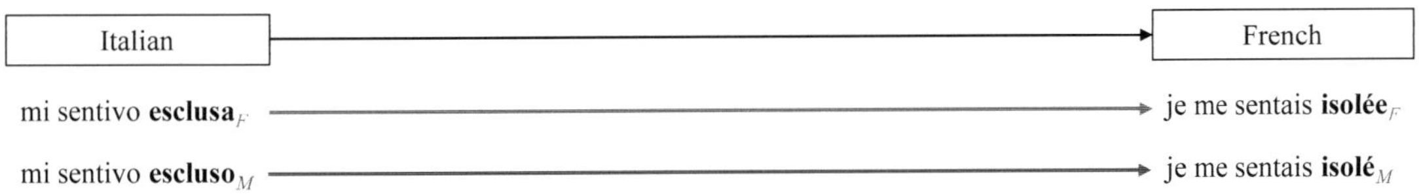

(a) Illustration of the translation between grammatical gender languages (Italian↔French) examined in this work; here, for Italian→French translation of the utterance "I felt alienated". Information necessary to disambiguate gender (bold) was always conveyed by the source sentence (here, in Italian) and to be reflected in the translation (here, in French).

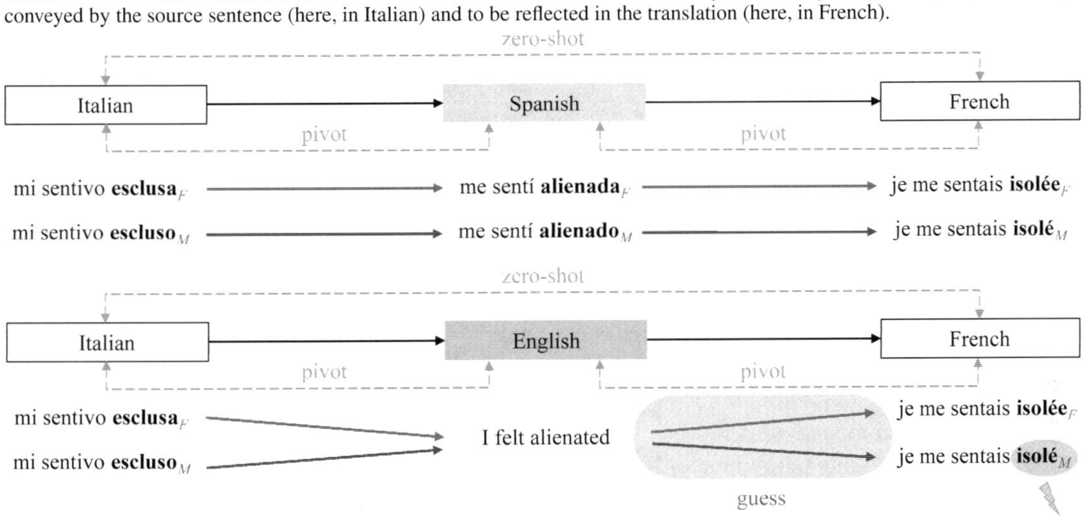

(b) The richness of the gender-inflectional system of the bridge language, used to facilitate translation for unseen language pairs, affects models' ability to preserve the gender information from the source sentence. Scarcity of gender inflection in the bridge language (e.g., English) causes models to miss gender clues from the source and to resort to guessing the gender; when making the wrong guess, i.e., choosing the wrong gender as presented in the source, the model exhibits gender hallucination.

Figure 1: Overview of our investigated translation scenario (here, for the utterance meaning "I felt alienated"): At inference, we translated between unseen gender-inflected source-target language pairs (i.e., Italian↔French) by bridging, implicitly (zero-shot) and explicitly (pivot-based), using bridge languages with different gender-inflectional systems (e.g., Spanish or English).

for additional context information for training or inference, Basta et al. (2020) concatenate each sentence with its predecessor to achieve slight improvements in gender translation. Moryossef et al. (2019) inject context information as they prepend a short phrase, e.g., "*she* said to *them*", to the source sentence, translate the sentence with the prefix, and afterward remove the prefix translation from the model's output. Specifying gender inflection in this way improves models' ability to generate feminine target forms, but it relies on (not always available) metadata about speakers and listeners. Furthermore, different gender-specific translations in terms of word choices can be an arguably non-desirable side-effect.

A different approach is to post-process the output using counterfactual data augmentation. Saunders and Byrne (2020) use a lattice rescoring module that maps gender-marked words in the output to all possible inflectional variants and rescores all paths in the lattice corresponding to the different sentences with a model that has been gender-biased at the cost of lower translation quality. Choosing the sentence with the highest score as the final translation results in increased accuracy of gender selection. A downside is that data augmentation is very demanding for complex sentences with a variety of gender phenomena, such as those typically occurring in natural language scenarios.

3 Analyzing Gender Bias in MNMT

In our experimental setting, information necessary to disambiguate gender was *always* conveyed by the source sentence (cf. Figure 1a) and, thus, available to the models. Motivated by our research inquiry, we focused our investigation on the effect of bridging on gender preservation in MNMT between unseen language pairs, as illustrated broadly in Figure 1b, exploring three influencing factors to learn about the cause-and-effect relationship of gender bias in MNMT: *i)* the approach taken to bridge unseen language pairs (i.e., using continuous representations for zero-shot translation or discrete pivot language representations); *ii)* the choice of bridge language; and *iii)* language-agnostic model hidden representations.

Zero-Shot Translation Vs. Pivoting: To bridge the gap between an unknown source-target language pair at inference, we took two different approaches using the same trained translation model. For *pivot-based translation*, we cascaded a model to perform source→pivot and pivot→target translation. As such, pivoting used the pivot language as an explicit bridge between the unknown language pair. For *zero-shot translation*, we used the same model to translate directly between the unknown language pair, relying on the model's learned semantic space where sentences with the same meaning are mapped to similar regions regardless of the language. Compared to pivoting, zero-shot translation circumvents error propagation and reduces computation time, but achieving high-quality zero-shot translations is challenging. In light of our inquiry, we analyzed each approach's ability to preserve gender, comparing their performances for the feminine and the masculine gender.[4]

Bridge Language: English often participates in most, if not all, language pairs in a training corpus, making English, a language limited to pronominal gender (with a few exceptions), the most reasonable choice for a bridge language. When translating into a genderless language (e.g., Hungarian), the potential loss of gender information conveyed by the source sentence is unproblematic as it is evidently without detrimental consequence. However, when translating into a language with a *higher* gender-inflected system than English (e.g., French or Italian), the loss of gender information poses a significant problem since the information necessary to disambiguate gender is virtually no longer existent (cf. bottom in Figure 1b).

As preserving non-existent gender information is inherently impossible, also for humans, it is fair to assume that MT models have difficulty when encountering this phenomenon of gender ambiguity; the simplest solution is to resort to *random guessing*, with a 50% chance of choosing one gender over the other. Any other gender distribution ($\neq$ 50:50%) is not reflective of random guessing but instead indicative of *educated guessing* based on knowledge or observations *assumed* to be true that can, however, include biases.

Against this background, we studied the role of the bridge language in gender preservation, focusing on the gender bias differences between pivot-based and zero-shot translation, using bridge languages with different gender-inflectional systems, including English (low gender inflection), German and Spanish (high(er) gender inflection). German and English are both Germanic languages. Whereas in German, all noun classes require masculine, feminine, or neuter[5] inflection, English lacks a similar grammatical gender system. In German, the gender of the noun is reflected in determiners like articles, possessives, and demonstratives. On the other hand, Spanish is a Romance language with a binary grammatical gender system, differentiating masculine and feminine nouns; from a grammatical point of view, there are no gender-neutral nouns. The gender of nouns agrees with (some) determiners and, more often than in German, adjectives, making gender a pervasive feature in Spanish.

Language-Agnostic Hidden Representations: Since languages are characterized by different linguistic features, including those related to gender, it is reasonable to assume that language-*specific* representations, tailored to the language pairs included during training, *impair* gender preservation for unseen language pairs. Because of this, we explored the effect of three modifications to (the training of) a baseline Transformer (Vaswani et al., 2017) to encourage language-*agnostic* hidden representations, which have proven to cause performance gains for zero-shot translation. We

- removed a residual connection in a middle Transformer encoder to *lessen positional correspondences to the input tokens* and, thereby, reduce dependencies to language-specific word order (R) as proposed by Liu et al. (2021),
- encouraged *similar (i.e., closer) source and target language representations* through an auxiliary loss (AUX_{SIM}) similar to Pham et al. (2019) and Arivazhagan et al. (2019), and
- performed joint adversarial training *penalizing recovery of source language signals* in the

[4] In the presentation of our results, we use ZS and PV, short for zero-shot and pivot-based translation when space is limited.

[5] In German, neuter gender inflection does not apply to nouns identifying people (cf. referential gender).

representations (ADV_{LAN}) as done by Arivazhagan et al. (2019).

In our experiments, we examined the effect of these three modifications in isolation and tested some combinations; in total, we compared five different models to our baseline (B)—which we refer to as $B{+}AUX_{SIM}$, $B{+}ADV_{LAN}$, R, $R{+}AUX_{SIM}$, and $R{+}ADV_{LAN}$—to determine whether they mitigated models' gender biases.

4 Evaluation Data & Procedure

For our evaluation, we built on the work of Bentivogli et al. (2020) regarding the data and procedure used for our gender bias evaluation.

4.1 Multilingual Gender Preservation Dataset

In our experiments, we used the publicly available TED-based corpora MuST-C (Di Gangi et al., 2019) for model training (cf. Section 5.1 for details) and evaluated our models on a subset of MuST-SHE (Bentivogli et al., 2020), a gender-annotated benchmark. MuST-SHE is a subset of MuST-C and is available for English-French, English-Italian, and English-Spanish translations, where at least one English gender-neutral word in a sentence needs to be translated into the corresponding masculine/feminine target word(s).

The target languages included in MuST-SHE allowed us to investigate gender preservation for sentences where *the source language always provides enough information to disambiguate gender*; with this research inquiry, two main criteria needed to be met by the evaluation data: First, we wanted to evaluate gender translation *between* grammatical gender languages. Therefore, we formed a many-to-many subset from MuST-SHE, keeping only true-parallel data and realigning it to support evaluating translation between the three initial target languages. Second, we wanted to investigate the gender biases in translation between language pairs unseen during training (i.e., zero-shot directions). Using training corpora comprising different language pairs, we built models with different supervised translation directions. Accordingly, the models did not share the same zero-shot directions. For instance, a model trained on Spanish-X data had seen examples for language pairs that included Spanish. Therefore, we discarded the Spanish examples and only used French-Italian examples in our evaluation to ensure equal zero-shot directions across all models considered in our experiments.

We obtained 278 sentences with detailed statistics presented in Table 1. The included French↔Italian directions left us with 556 translations for evaluation.

	Feminine (Female/Male)		Masculine (Female/Male)		**Total** (Female/Male)	
Cat. 1	64	(64/0)	56	(0/56)	120	(64/56)
Cat. 2	72	(58/14)	86	(27/59)	158	(85/73)
Total	136	(122/14)	142	(27/115)	**278**	(149/129)

Table 1: Statistics of the MuST-SHE data used, broken down by referent gender (Feminine/Masculine), gender agreement (Cat. 1/2: speaker-related/speaker-independent), and speaker gender (Female/Male).

The composition of this dataset, comprising French-Italian parallel data, provides different evaluative dimensions that can be considered for gender bias evaluation of MT models.

Referent Gender: Grammatical gender agreement determines the modification of certain words to express gender congruent with the other words they relate to, which, in our case, were the words designating a *referent*—a person the speaker mentioned. Consequently, the gender of a referent (cf. referential gender) determined the gender of gender-marked words relating to the referent (i.e., for a female referent, feminine inflected words, and for a male referent, masculine inflections). All gender-marked words in a sentence did agree with the same (referent) gender. As MuST-SHE is TED-based data, a referent was either the speaker, or a person not identified as the speaker (nor the addressee(s)/audience in our data).

Speaker Gender: Due to the evaluation data stemming from TED talks, examples are transcribed utterances spoken by different speakers of both feminine or masculine gender. Depending on the type of gender agreement occurring in an utterance, the speaker's gender and referents' gender did or did not correlate.

Gender Agreement: Whenever the speaker was the referent, i.e., the speaker was referring to him- or herself, there is speaker-*related* gender agreement among those gender-marked words referring to the speaker. Languages with a less pronounced inflection of gender, such as English, can encounter syntactic structures that do not indicate a speaker's gender (cf. bottom in Figure 1b). In contrast, syntactic structures of languages with rich gender-inflected systems typically encode enough information to unambiguously classify a speaker's gender (cf. top in Figure 1b). Consequently, we hypothesized that using English as a bridge language results in the loss of gender information for sentences with speaker-related gender agreement; meanwhile, the higher gender-inflected grammatical gender languages, German and Spanish, were hypothesized to preserve the gender information when used as a bridge language.

Whenever a person other than the speaker was the referent, i.e., the speaker was talking about someone else (e.g., "mi *padre* se sentía alienado$_M$" = "my dad felt alienated" uttered by a *female* speaker), there is speaker-*independent* gender agreement among those gender-marked words referring to the referent. For these examples in our data, meaning construction typically does not require the integration of semantic information about the speaker for correct syntactic processing and translation. The gender inflection of words is therefore often purely based on syntactic agreement with a formally marked subject (here, the referent), making the referent's gender identity explicit in those utterances for all three considered bridge languages, English, German, and Spanish.

4.2 Method of Measurement

Similar to Bentivogli et al. (2020), we used the concept of gender-swapping to measure how often a model preserved the gender compared to how often it produced the opposite gender form, thus opting for the wrong instead of the correct gender, which, if frequently done, signaled models' acting on gender biases.

Following this idea, models' generated translations of gender-marked words belonged to one of three categories, which we exemplify using Figure 2. First, the *expected translation*, for which we measured how often the *correct* translation (ground truth)—specified by a reference translation C-REF—was produced (e.g., "isolée" in the exemplary model output in Figure 2). Second, the *gender-reversed translation*, for which we measured how often the translation was *wrong*, but only regarding the gender inflection of gender-marked words—specified by a reference W-REF—i.e., instead of the required correct gender realization as per ground truth (e.g., the feminine adjective "intimidée"), the model produced the opposite gender form (e.g., the masculine adjective "intimidé"). Third, a *translation different from both reference translations*, e.g., instead of "jugée" (C-REF) or "jugé" (W-REF), the model produced the adjective "condamnée", or any other word not matching C-REF or W-REF; in this case, we had no reference as to whether the gender inflection, regardless of the predicted word base, was correct or wrong, forcing us to exclude these translations from our gender bias evaluation.

We used two metrics to evaluate our models: BLEU (similar to Bentivogli et al. (2020)) and accuracy. For the accuracy on feminine and masculine word forms, we measured how often a model was able to produce the correct gender (C) for those words that matched either the correct or the wrong reference set (C+W); we refer to this as *gender preservation* (α_{correct}). As we only relied on correct and wrong "matches" (C+W)—excluding words that did not match any reference set (N)—the larger in size this set was, i.e., the larger the sample size, the more significant our findings; therefore, we weighted α_{correct} by the size of C+W in relation to the number of all translations (C+W+N), matching a reference (C+W) or not matching any reference (N); we refer to this weighting factor as *sample size* (ρ). Formally, we defined the accuracy γ to measure the *gender preservation performance weighted by the sample size* as follows:

$$\gamma = \underbrace{\frac{C}{C+W}}_{\alpha_{\text{correct}}} \cdot \underbrace{\frac{C+W}{C+W+N}}_{\rho} = \frac{C}{C+W+N}$$

To compare the performances for the two genders, we computed the *gender gap* δ between results for feminine and the masculine word forms:

$$\delta = 1 - \frac{\min(\gamma^{\text{F}}, \gamma^{\text{M}})}{\max(\gamma^{\text{F}}, \gamma^{\text{M}})}$$

As a reflection of gender biases, gender gaps should be as small as possible and ideally zero due to minimal differences between the results for the feminine and the masculine gender. Furthermore, we analyzed the difference between scores for the correct and the wrong references to determine whether translations were gender-biased.

5 Experiments & Results

The code and scripts used for our experimental evaluation are available on GitHub.[6]

[6]https://github.com/lenacabrera/gb_mnmt

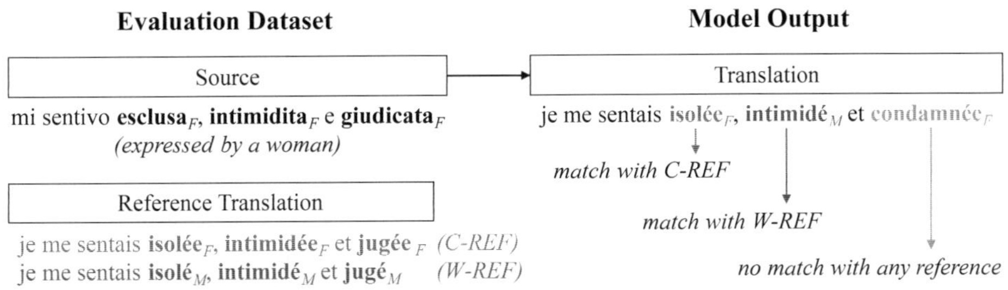

Figure 2: Illustration of the three possible translation outcomes of required gender preservation for Italian→French translation of the utterance "I felt *alienated*, *intimidated*, and *judged*": The translation of a gender-inflected word either matched the correct reference translation *C-REF* (here, "isolée" = alienated), the wrong reference translation *W-REF* (here, "intimidé" = intimidated), or neither (here, "condamnée" = condemned).

5.1 Experimental Setup

Training Data: In our experiments, we used the publicly available corpora MuST-C (Di Gangi et al., 2019) for model training. To investigate the impact of the bridge language, determined by the language pairs included during training, we formed three training corpora that are subsets of MuST-C (X),[7] with language pairs en↔X\en, de↔X\de, and es↔X\es, where X\en is the language set X excluding English (en), German (de), or Spanish (es). On each of the three corpora, we trained a model and afterward evaluated the three trained models on our evaluation data. Since only a portion (~10%) of MuST-C is true-parallel data, the training corpora differed in size, as specified in Table 2.

Language Pairs	# Sentences per Direction
en ↔ X\en	125,000–267,000
de ↔ X\de	103,000–223,000
es ↔ X\es	102,000–258,000

Table 2: Overview of the three MuST-C subsets used.

Preprocessing: MuST-C comes with partitioned training and validation sets which we kept unchanged in our experiments, except for the modifications described above. For the training and validation data, we first performed tokenization and truecasing using the Moses[8] tokenizer and truecaser. Afterward, we learned byte pair encoding (BPE) using subword-nmt[9] (Sennrich et al., 2016). We performed 20 thousand merge operations and only used tokens occurring in the training set with a minimum frequency of 50 times. Our evaluation data was preprocessed in a similar way using the BPE-learned vocabulary.

Training & Inference Details: Our baseline was a Transformer with 5 encoder and 5 decoder layers with 8 attention heads, an embedding size of 512, and an inner size of 2048. For regularization, we used dropout with a rate of 0.2 and performed label smoothing with a rate of 0.1. Moreover, we used the learning rate schedule from Vaswani et al. (2017) with 8,000 warmup steps (WUS). The source and target word embeddings were shared. To specify the output language, we used a target-language-specific beginning-of-sentence token. As part of our model modifications, we removed a residual connection (R) in the third encoder layer (Liu et al., 2021). We trained each model for 64 epochs and averaged the weights of the five best checkpoints ordered by the validation loss. For the auxiliary similarity loss (AUX_{SIM}) and the adversarial language classifier (ADV_{LAN}), we resumed training of the baseline and the model with removed residual connections for 10 additional epochs (400 WUS). By default, we only included supervised directions in the validation set. To compute BLEU scores, we used sacreBLEU (Post, 2018), which provides a fair and reproducible evaluation, as it operates on detokenized text.

5.2 Results

In Figure 3, we present the BLEU scores indicative of the similarity of the generated translations of MuST-SHE utterances to the *Correct* references and their gender-reversed counterparts (*Wrong* references) regardless of the referent gender, as well as the difference (delta) between *Cor-*

[7]From release version 1.2, we included 10 of the 15 available languages: Czech, Dutch, English, French, German, Italian, Portuguese, Romanian, Russian, and Spanish.

[8]https://github.com/moses-smt/mosesdecoder

[9]https://github.com/rsennrich/subword-nmt

rect and *Wrong* scores for zero-shot models only.[10]

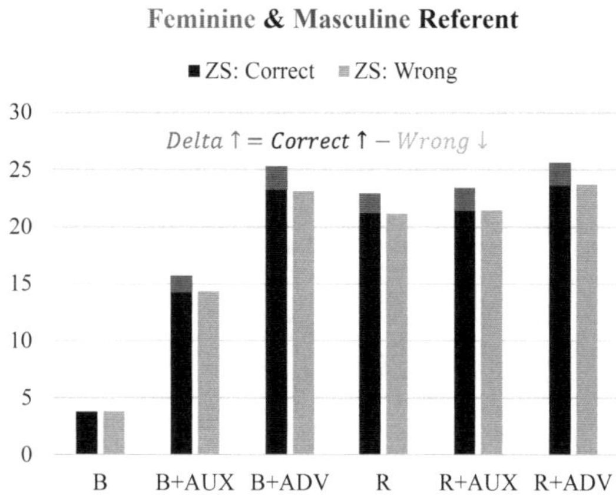

Figure 3: Average BLEU scores for *Correct* (left bar, higher ↑ is better) and *Wrong* (right bar, lower ↓ is better) MuST-SHE references of our six evaluated zero-shot models, complemented with the delta (green bar, higher ↑ is better) between both. Results are for the feminine and masculine referent gender.[10]

The bar graph illustrates that modifying our baseline B to encourage language-agnostic representations improves the poor gender preservation performance of B noticeably when performing zero-shot translation. While the delta between *Correct* and *Wrong* scores for B is zero, we consistently observe positive deltas (cf. green bars) that signal more correct than wrong gender translations; hence, through more language-agnostic hidden representations the modified zero-shot models more often can recover information (conveyed by the source language sentence) necessary to preserve the gender in the target language translation which, in turn, reduces the number of translations produced based on reflecting learned gender biases (in response to RQ3). It shows that $R+ADV_{LAN}$, closely followed by $B+ADV_{LAN}$, yields the highest *Correct* BLEU scores (higher is better) and one of the largest deltas between *Correct* and *Wrong* scores (higher is better); therefore, we take a closer look at the performance of $R+ADV_{LAN}$.

Complementary to the BLEU-based evaluation, we examine $R+ADV_{LAN}$ accuracies (γ), where better or worse performance measured is reliably attributed to better or worse translation of *gender-inflected words only*. From Figure 4, we can observe very similar performances for zero-shot and pivot-based translation using $R+ADV_{LAN}$ (RQ1). While both approaches achieve similar

[10]Results are for models trained on en↔X\en data.

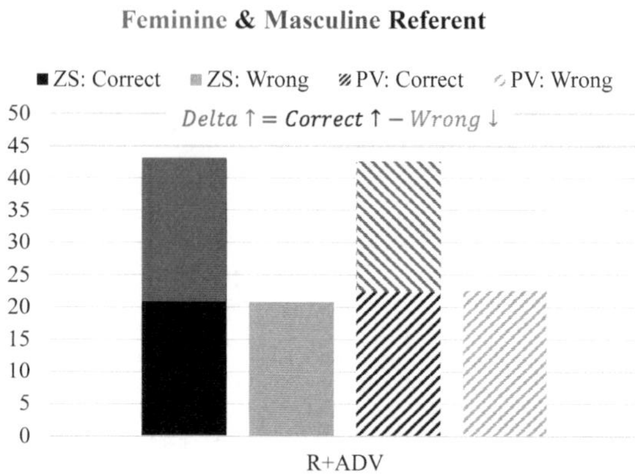

Figure 4: Average accuracy scores of zero-shot translation (full bars) and pivoting (hatched) for *Correct* (left bar, higher ↑ is better) and *Wrong* (right bar, lower ↓ is better) MuST-SHE references complemented with the delta (green bars, higher ↑ is better) between both for the model $R+ADV_{LAN}$. Results are for the feminine and masculine referent gender.[10]

Correct accuracy scores (43.0 for ZS and 42.5 for PV), we observe slightly lower *Wrong* scores for zero-shot translation (20.8) than for pivoting (22.5). As a result, the delta for zero-shot is higher (better) than for pivot-based translation (22.2 vs. 20.2).

To gain better insight into the difference in gender preservation between both approaches, we break down the accuracies and compare them for the feminine and masculine gender; the corresponding results are depicted in Figure 5. The large differences between the accuracies for feminine and masculine referents clearly show that the model is acting according to a *masculine bias* that detriments feminine and benefits masculine preservation of gender signals conveyed by the source sentence. The *Correct* accuracies in the masculine case are almost twice as high as their feminine counterparts. Furthermore, comparing the *Wrong* accuracies, we see an even bigger difference, as masculine *Wrong* scores are much smaller (by a factor of 5), whereas feminine *Wrong* scores are almost identical to their *Correct* counterparts.

In the masculine case, performances by both approaches are very similar, with pivoting achieving slightly higher *Correct* and *Wrong* scores (54.5 vs. 53.4 and 10.6 vs. 10.4). In the feminine case, we see that zero-shot translation is more accurate regarding feminine gender preservation: The delta between *Correct* and *Wrong* accuracies is small but positive (0.5), whereas for pivoting, we observe a negative delta (-4.9) that signals more wrong (masculine) than correct (feminine) trans-

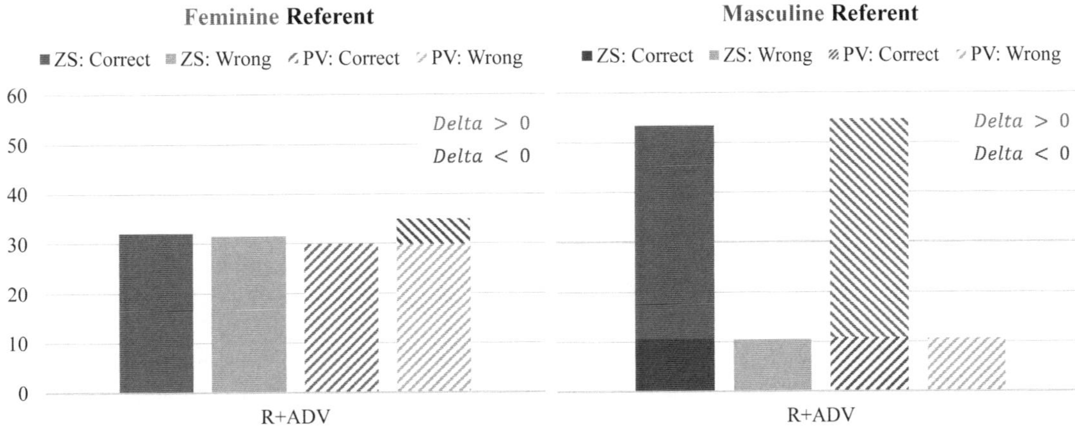

Figure 5: Average accuracy scores of zero-shot translation (full bars) and pivoting (hatched) for *Correct* (left bar, higher ↑ is better) and *Wrong* (right bar, lower ↓ is better) MuST-SHE references, complemented with the delta (green [$Delta > 0$] and magenta [$Delta < 0$] bars, higher ↑ is better) between both for the model $R + ADV_{LAN}$. Results are broken down by referent gender (feminine [left] vs. masculine [right]).[10]

lations for words where the required gender realization is feminine. Accordingly, it turns out that zero-shot translation performs noticeably better for feminine gender preservation—which is generally poorer than masculine gender preservation—compared to pivoting and, as a consequence, mitigates the masculine biases to a larger extent, producing more balanced gender outputs (RQ1).

As we assumed the bridge language to play an important role in gender preservation, we compare the model's performance for zero-shot and pivot-based translation when trained using different training corpora that enabled the use of different bridge languages, namely English (for the results presented so far) and the grammatical gender languages German and Spanish (in response to RQ2). As we expected to see differences between the three languages regarding sentences with and without speaker-related gender agreement, we present the *Correct* accuracies broken down by referent gender and complemented with the gender gap (δ) between feminine and masculine accuracies for either utterance category in Table 3.

Bridge Language	Feminine ↑		Masculine ↑		**Gender Gap ↓**	
	ZS	PV	ZS	PV	ZS	PV
	Speaker-*Independent* Gender Agreement					
English	42.8	39.8	56.7	**58.3**	0.25	0.32
German	40.4	43.6	50.1	55.6	0.19	0.22
Spanish	**49.6**	45.3	57.7	55.0	**0.14**	0.18
	Speaker-*Related* Gender Agreement					
English	20.2	19.2	48.2	48.7	0.58	0.61
German	15.1	18.4	**51.1**	49.8	0.70	0.63
Spanish	23.8	**29.4**	50.6	45.7	0.53	**0.36**

Table 3: Average accuracy scores for *Correct* (higher ↑ is better) references with speaker-related and speaker-independent gender agreement when bridging via English, German or Spanish using the model $R + ADV_{LAN}$. Results are broken down by referent gender and complemented with the gender gap (lower ↓ is better) between feminine and masculine accuracies. Underlined scores are the best of both approaches, and bold scores are the best across languages.

It shows that the performances for speaker-independent gender agreement are noticeably better (i.e., higher accuracies and smaller gender gaps) than for speaker-related gender agreement, which can be attributed to reduced gender ambiguity due to more explicit gender clues provided by source sentences in the former case. It shows that the poorer performance for speaker-related gender agreement affects the feminine gender more than the masculine gender when considering the much smaller difference in results for masculine word forms compared to a significant drop in scores for feminine word forms for speaker-related gender agreement (again, this very prominently highlights the model's masculine bias). Consequently, it shows that the feminine discrimination found throughout all models' performances is more prominent in cases of high gender ambiguity, confirming the notion of models making "educated" gender guesses that are tainted by gender biases.

Moreover, our results reveal clear differences in gender preservation between languages for both types of gender agreement: For speaker-independent gender agreement (e.g., "mi *padre* se sentía alienado$_M$" = "my dad felt alienated"), we find that zero-shot translation produces smaller gender gaps compared to pivoting for all three bridge languages. For the English bridge, the difference between zero-shot translation and pivoting is most pronounced, albeit small. For speaker-related gender agreement (e.g., "me sentí alienada$_F$" = "I felt alienated"), it turns out that zero-shot translation achieves a slightly smaller gender gap compared to pivoting using the English bridge language (where gender information is likely lost); for the German and the Spanish bridge languages, we observe better pivoting results regarding smaller gender gaps and, thus, more balanced correct gender outputs. This outcome confirms our hypothesis that for languages where gender inflection is relatively low, zero-shot translation is not as much affected by a loss of gender information (which impairs gender preservation for pivoting using discrete language representations), as it relies on more language-agnostic gender clues likely found in the continuous representations. Moreover, the outcomes suggest that with an increased level of gender inflection in the bridge language, pivoting surpasses zero-shot translation regarding fairly balanced gender preservation for speaker-related gender agreement.

6 Conclusion

In this paper, we explored gender bias in MNMT in the context of gender preservation for zero-shot translation directions, i.e., unseen language pairs (French↔Italian), compared the performances of pivoting and zero-shot translation using discrete and continuous representations respectively, studied the influence the bridge language has on both approaches, and examined the effect language-agnostic representations have on zero-shot models' gender biases. Based on our experimental results, we addressed three research questions.

RQ1 How do zero-shot and pivot-based translation compare regarding gender-biased outputs for zero-shot directions?

We find that zero-shot translation and pivoting achieve similar gender preservation performances, but zero-shot translation better preserves the feminine gender, which mitigates the masculine bias—the consistently worse feminine than masculine results across all evaluated models and both approaches—more than pivoting when bridging via English.

RQ2 Does the bridge language affect the gender biases perpetuated by zero-shot and pivot-based translations?

Our experiments revealed that the bridge language affects gender biases in MNMT. For English, a language limited to pronominal gender (with a few exceptions), we find that zero-shot translation performs better than pivoting regarding a more fairly balanced preservation of feminine and masculine gender. Using two richer gender-inflected bridge languages, Spanish and German, revealed that with an increased level of gender inflection in the bridge language, pivoting surpasses zero-shot translation regarding fewer gender-biased outputs for utterances with speaker-related gender agreement.

RQ3 Do translation quality improvements of zero-shot models reduce their gender biases?

All three evaluated modifications encouraging language-agnostic hidden representations (cf. Section 3) improved zero-shot models' ability to preserve the feminine and masculine gender and reduced the gap between better masculine and worse feminine results; they improved zero-shot models' performances to the point where they outperformed pivoting regarding more fairly balanced preservation of both genders when bridging via English.

Besides our findings, this work also features some limitations that can be addressed in future work. First, the data used in our experimental evaluation limited the scenarios to those examined. Future work can examine the translation of sentences with mixed gender (i.e., sentences including feminine *and* masculine word forms) and directions, including languages from different language families and with different gender systems, to further study language differences. Second, developing a large-scale gender-annotated corpus suitable for MNMT training could most likely be used to improve models' gender preservation performance. A well-performing gender classifier could be used to annotate the MuST-C dataset with token- or word-level gender labels. Third, we believe that the metrics currently used to evaluate models' gender biases are not ideal. For instance, model outputs mismatching the reference translations used for evaluation are discarded, despite potentially being appropriate translations (e.g., synonyms); future work could explore using additional morphological analysis tools to include those translations in the gender bias evaluation. Generally, inquiring about the phenomenon of gender bias in translation requires appropriate and established metrics; the lack thereof currently leaves room for improvement in evaluative procedures.

While there is a lot of potential for further research on this topic, it is crucial to acknowledge that, ultimately, translation technology is bound by the principles of language, which subtly reproduces societal asymmetries and embeds signs of sexism, including masculine defaults and more subtle conventions by which expressions referring to females are grammatically more complex in many languages. Consequently, combating gender biases in translation technology requires awareness of language use, as it is one of the most powerful means through which sexism and gender discrimination are perpetrated and reproduced.

References

Ackerman, Lauren M. 2019. Syntactic and cognitive issues in investigating gendered coreference. *Glossa*.

Arivazhagan, Naveen, Ankur Bapna, Orhan Firat, Roee Aharoni, Melvin Johnson, and Wolfgang Macherey. 2019. The missing ingredient in zero-shot neural machine translation. *arXiv preprint arXiv:1903.07091*.

Basta, Christine, Marta R Ruiz Costa-jussà, and José Adrián Rodríguez Fonollosa. 2020. Towards mitigating gender bias in a decoder-based neural machine translation model by adding contextual information. In *Proceedings of the 4th Widening Natural Language Processing Workshop*, pages 99–102, Online.

Bentivogli, Luisa, Beatrice Savoldi, Matteo Negri, Mattia Antonino Di Gangi, Roldano Cattoni, and Marco Turchi. 2020. Gender in danger? Evaluating speech translation technology on the MuST-SHE corpus. *arXiv preprint arXiv:2006.05754*.

Cao, Yang Trista and Hal Daumé III. 2021. Toward gender-inclusive coreference resolution: An analysis of gender and bias throughout the machine learning lifecycle. *Computational Linguistics*, 47(3):615–661, November.

Corbett, Greville. 1991. *Gender*. Cambridge University Press.

Di Gangi, Mattia A., Roldano Cattoni, Luisa Bentivogli, Matteo Negri, and Marco Turchi. 2019. MuST-C: a Multilingual Speech Translation Corpus. In *Proceedings of the 2019 Conference of the North American Chapter of the Association for Computational Linguistics: Human Language Technologies*, volume 1 (Long and Short Papers), pages 2012–2017, Minneapolis, Minnesota.

Liu, Danni, Jan Niehues, James Cross, Francisco Guzmán, and Xian Li. 2021. Improving zero-shot translation by disentangling positional information. In *Proceedings of the 59th Annual Meeting of the Association for Computational Linguistics and the 11th International Joint Conference on Natural Language Processing (Volume 1: Long Papers)*, pages 1259–1273, Online.

Moryossef, Amit, Roee Aharoni, and Yoav Goldberg. 2019. Filling gender & number gaps in neural machine translation with black-box context injection. *arXiv preprint arXiv:1903.03467*.

Pham, Ngoc-Quan, Jan Niehues, Thanh-Le Ha, and Alex Waibel. 2019. Improving zero-shot translation with language-independent constraints. In *Proceedings of the 4th Conference on Machine Translation. Vol. 1. Ed.: O. Bojar*, pages 13–23.

Post, Matt. 2018. A call for clarity in reporting BLEU scores. In *Proceedings of the 3rd Conference on Machine Translation: Research Papers*, pages 186–191, Brussels, Belgium.

Saunders, Danielle and Bill Byrne. 2020. Reducing gender bias in neural machine translation as a domain adaptation problem. *arXiv preprint arXiv:2004.04498*.

Savoldi, Beatrice, Marco Gaido, Luisa Bentivogli, Matteo Negri, and Marco Turchi. 2021. Gender bias in machine translation. *Transactions of the Association for Computational Linguistics*, 9:845–874.

Sennrich, Rico, Barry Haddow, and Alexandra Birch. 2016. Neural machine translation of rare words with subword units. In *Proceedings of the 54th Annual Meeting of the Association for Computational Linguistics*, volume 1, pages 1715–1725, Berlin, Germany.

Vanmassenhove, Eva, Christian Hardmeier, and Andy Way. 2018. Getting gender right in neural machine translation. In *Proceedings of the 2018 Conference on Empirical Methods in Natural Language Processing*, pages 3003–3008, Brussels, Belgium.

Vaswani, Ashish, Noam Shazeer, Niki Parmar, Jakob Uszkoreit, Llion Jones, Aidan N Gomez, Łukasz Kaiser, and Illia Polosukhin. 2017. Attention is all you need. In *Advances in Neural Information Processing Systems*, volume 30, pages 5998–6008.

Gender-inclusive translation for a gender-inclusive sport: strategies and translator perceptions at the International Quadball Association

Joke Daems
Ghent University
joke.daems@ugent.be
International Quadball Association
joke.daems@iqasport.org

Abstract

Gender-inclusive language is of key importance to the IQA, the international governing body for quadball, a mixed-gender contact sport that explicitly welcomes players of all genders. While relatively straightforward for English, the picture becomes more complicated for most of the other IQA working languages. This paper provides an overview of the strategies currently chosen by translation team leaders for different IQA languages, the factors that influenced this decision and their connection with existing research on inclusive language strategies. It further explores the awareness and attitudes of IQA translators towards those strategies and factors.

1 Introduction

Quadball is a mixed-gender, full-contact sport played around the world. A quadball team consists of up to 21 athletes with seven players per team on the field at any one time. The IQA is the international governing body for quadball, representing 19 National Governing Bodies (NGBs) with Full Member status and 19 NGBs with Associate Member status at the time of writing. The IQA organizes international events, offers support to its members, and promotes the sport and its values of gender equity and inclusivity. The sport's rulebook explicitly acknowledges players of all genders: "All quadball athletes have the right to define how they identify and it is this stated gender that is recognized on pitch" (6) and enforces the presence of multiple genders on pitch via the so called 'gender maximum rule': "A team may not have more than four players who identify as the same gender in play at the same time" (11).

Because of the importance of gender inclusivity, all IQA publications (e.g., the rulebook, policies, and reports) are written using gender-inclusive language. As IQA documents are drafted in English, a natural gender language, this is achieved relatively straightforwardly by avoiding gender-specific nouns and using the pronouns 'they/them' when referring to a person of unknown gender. Increasingly, however, the IQA translation team is trying to provide core content (i.e., the rulebook and referee tests) in languages other than English. At the time of writing, there are translators working into 8 languages: Catalan, Dutch, French, German, Italian, Portuguese, Spanish, and Turkish. Given the unique nature of each language and the fact that the translation teams consist of (an often limited number of) volunteers, gender-inclusive language is implemented to different degrees for each target language.

This paper provides an overview of the different strategies currently in use at the IQA, the factors that influenced those strategies, and a discussion of the strategy compared to existing research on gender-inclusive writing for that language (if available). This is followed by a report on a survey conducted among the IQA translators, exploring their awareness of inclusive language strategies, their attitudes towards them and the factors that influence the choice of strategy. The paper concludes with some key findings and plans for future work.

2 Related work

Quite a large body of work has indicated that the use of certain linguistic forms leads to certain mental representations with, for example, the supposedly 'generic' masculine evoking a male bias in readers' minds (Stahlberg et al., 2007). A possible way of countering these biases is by using gender-fair language, which has "the potential to make significant contributions to the reduction of gender stereotyping and discrimination" (Sczesny et al., 2016). However, while women were found to use more gender-fair language after being exposed to a text containing such language, men needed to be made explicitly aware of this language use before using it themselves (Koeser et al., 2015).

Until relatively recently, most of the work on gender-fair language focused on masculine and feminine genders only, but society and research now increasingly acknowledge the importance of non-binary gender identities. As "[r]epresentation in language can be very important to one's ability to have their identity understood by others and recognized in everyday speech interactions" (Hord, 2016), the use of gender-inclusive or gender neutral language is on the rise. There are a variety of strategies to include non-binary identities in language. López (2022) divides them into two main groups: Indirect Non-binary Language (INL), where gender markers are avoided altogether, and Direct Non-binary Language (DNL), where linguistic innovation takes place to make non-binary identities explicitly visible. Often, a combination of those strategies is suggested, with Kosnick (2019) acknowledging that "[l]everaging non-binary language [...] in ways that do not deviate from current linguistic norms is one productive strategy" and that it can be combined with neologisms or neopronouns to allow for "linguistic possibilities through which non-binary speakers/writers can more authentically articulate their experiences and, thereby, come to exist in language" (152). However, the use and acceptance of such language greatly depends on the language itself, with natural gender languages being more open to linguistic changes than grammatical gender languages (Hord, 2016).

This imbalance between languages when it comes to gender-inclusivity potentially creates challenges in translation, particularly when translating from a natural gender language like English into heavily grammatically gendered languages like French or Spanish. In a paper discussing audiovisual translation and representation of non-binary characters, López (2022) shows how characters' gender identity can get lost in translation and argues that it is a translator's "responsibility to keep non-binary people visible" (232). According to Attig (2022), working on similar data, translators need to have "an awareness of and engagement with the ever-evolving culture of the community one is translating" (14). In the most comprehensive survey on gender-fair (machine) translation to date, Lardelli and Gromann (2023) argue that there is no one-size-fits-all solution when it comes to determining gender-fair language strategy in translation due to its complexity and context-specificity. From these perspectives, the translation department of the IQA offers an ideal use case, as most translators are active members of the quadball community themselves, and are thus very aware of the context in which their translations will appear.

3 Gender-inclusive translation strategies at the IQA

Of the 8 IQA working languages, there is one genderless language (Turkish), requiring no additional strategies for gender inclusivity in translation. The other languages express gender grammatically to different degrees: Dutch is a grammatical gender language that is gradually becoming a natural gender language like English; Catalan, French, Italian, Portuguese, and Spanish are masculine-feminine gender languages; and German is a masculine-feminine-neuter gender language. To get an idea of the chosen strategy for each language and the factors that influenced this decision, I contacted all translation team leaders via the official IQA Slack workspace. Some answered my questions via chat, others wrote out a document outlining the strategies and factors in more detail. The following section offers an – inevitably very condensed – overview per language, with the exception of Dutch[1].

3.1 Strategies and motivation per language

Catalan: The Catalan translation team is the smallest (two translators), yet it is very active. A variety of gender-inclusive strategies has been tested by the team over the years, and these have been followed by the Catalan NGB to different degrees, depending on the NGB board at the time:

- Doubling up ('desdoblament'), using both masculine and feminine endings (e.g., 'un/a jugador/a', 'uns/unes àrbitres'). Pro: also used in media and therefore recognizable, con: makes sentences harder to read.
- Plural feminine (e.g., 'les jugadores' instead of 'els jugadors'). Pro: easier to read, con: seen as presumptuous and disconnected from the community.
- Plural masculine with generic forms where possible (e.g., 'equip arbitral' instead of 'els àrbitres'). Pro: easier to read, con: can be seen to exclude women and non-binary people.

The last strategy is the strategy currently in use. The translation team leader is aware of the suggested use of the vowel 'i' as an ending to indicate non-binary people (Duarte, 2022), but argues that this is not actively being used in practice, could lead to misunderstandings of the rules, and that it is not a perfect

[1] The only Dutch translator currently working for the IQA is also the author of this paper, and it is a bit hard to interview oneself.

strategy for Catalan, given that there are masculine words ending in -i as well (e.g., 'empresari'). In general, the team leader is clearly aware of the complexities of the Catalan language and sociological background. He explicitly mentions wanting to read the work by Junyent (2021), and states: "I think it is important to be open to new ideas as society and languages change and I do believe that new gender-inclusive language strategies for Catalan could be developed and adopted in the future."

The book by Junyent (2021) collects opinions from a variety of linguists on the topic of gender-inclusivity in Catalan, inevitably leading to a broad spectrum: some linguists defend the use of the generic masculine by stating that grammatical gender is unrelated to biological sex or gender, others prefer the 'desdoblament' strategy to explicitly make women visible in language, and yet others say that this strategy does not work, either because it excludes non-binary people, or because by making the distinction between men and women explicit, we strengthen the idea that they are fundamentally different people and should therefore be treated differently.

French: The French translation team consists of approximately five translators. The size of the team is hard to measure accurately, as most translators work for the French NGB and collaborate with the IQA, but are not official IQA volunteers. The strategy currently in use by the French translation team is the use of the interpunct ('point médian') between the masculine and feminine endings of a word, and the use of the gender-inclusive pronoun 'iel' (instead of the masculine 'il' or feminine 'elle'), e.g., 'Si le·a joueur·euse entrant·e intéragit avec le jeu [...] iel doit être pénalisé·e'. Unfortunately, the team leader did not reply to my messages on Slack in time to add additional clarifications as to why and how this particular strategy was chosen.

Looking at recent research on gender-inclusive French, it does seem that the interpunct strategy is the dominant strategy. Inclusive writing is strongly opposed or even ridiculed in France, particularly by the conservative Académie française, generally on the grounds of its assumed pointlessness in making women more visible in language (the existence of non-binary people is rarely acknowledged in this discourse), its reduced readability and the idea that the language would become even harder to learn (Académie française, 2021; Manesse, 2022). However, the few studies that have actually looked at readability indicate that inclusive writing strategies are not harder to read than generic masculine (Girard et al., 2021) and that readers rapidly get used to new forms of writing (Liénardy et al., 2023). Compared to 'generic' masculine forms, gender-fair forms were also shown to increase the visibility of women (Liénardy et al., 2023; Tibblin et al., 2023).

German: The German team consists of six translators. Gender-inclusive translation strategies are used so that every member of the community can find themselves in the texts. Different team leaders preferred different strategies:

- Gender asterisk ('Gendersternchen') to include masculine and feminine forms of words, with the * indicating non-binary identities (e.g., 'ein*e deutschsprachige*r Spieler*in'), simplified in the rulebook translations to improve readability ('eine deutschsprachige Spieler*in').
- Gender colon and leaving English terms untranslated, forms written in full depending on the case (e.g., 'Ein:e rennende:r Chaser', 'Der Ball eines:einer Spielers:Spielerin', 'Ich gebe den Ball einem:einer Spieler:in').

The last strategy is the strategy currently in use. There was a discussion with the German-speaking NGBs (Austria, Germany, and Switzerland) to determine the strategy. Other symbols like the gender asterisk (*) and interpunct (·) were discussed as well. Given that Swiss translators already have to copy/paste the 'ß' symbol used in standard German, the interpunct was discarded because it is hard to type (and incompatible with the current IQA font). Other core factors in determining the strategy were readability and compatibility, and the fact that the colon is also increasingly being used by the media. The team leader was additionally informed by someone with a background in gender studies, offering access to relevant articles. The decision to no longer translate position names was influenced by readability, as well as the fact that referees use the English terms in practice. The English 'keeper zone' then becomes 'Keeper-Zone' rather than 'Hüter:innen-Zone'.

Recent research on the readability of gender-inclusive German strategies indicates that "the use of the gender asterisk tended to have a rather positive effect on subjective comprehensibility, word difficulty, and aesthetic appeal, and did not impair sentence difficulty", although the opposite was found when a text contained many singular nouns (Friedrich et al., 2021). The colon has been introduced more recently and has not been studied to the same extent yet, although its adoption seems potentially controversial and seems particularly opposed by the visually impaired, as it is less recognisable than the asterisk and can be more easily confused with a letter 'i' (bukof, 2022).

Italian: The Italian translation team consists of four members. The team leader is aware of different potential strategies (using a gender asterisk, replacing gendered endings with 'u', removing the last letter altogether) and favours the more recent proposition by activist Luca Boschetto and sociolinguist Vera Gheno to replace the last letter with the '-ə' (e.g., 'lə direttorə' instead of 'i direttori'). While the translation team already actively uses this strategy for smaller texts and documents, the team leader is reluctant to use the forms in larger documents like the rulebook. The main reason is that there is ongoing debate about the readability of these forms, particularly for people with dyslexia or other specific learning disabilities. As a current solution, the introduction, conclusion and changelog of the rulebook are written in the gender-inclusive language, while the main content chapters of the rulebook are written using alternatively feminine or masculine variants and pronouns. The team leader does believe in the importance of gender-inclusive translations and states that "if new and more functioning Italian neutral-forms will appear in the future I will be 100% happy to implement it".

Research confirms that a variety of linguistic strategies have been used in Italian, to varying degrees of success, with asterisks and the schwa currently being the most common, and endings like -x and -u being used to a lesser degree (Comandini, 2021). Such strategies are often met with resistance, either because they go against the internal structure of the language (De Santis, 2022) or because they might lead to readability issues, particularly for people with dyslexia (D'Achille, 2022). Some researchers argue that the more neutral endings render women invisible (Robustelli, 2021), or that the generic masculine should simply be seen as 'neutral' (D'Achille, 2022). Many of these arguments have been countered by Gheno (2022), stating that from an intersectional point of view it makes no sense to pit different kinds of diversities against each other (e.g. the rights of non-binary people in opposition to those of people with dyslexia), as this implies there is some sort of hierarchy of diversity rights, and it ignores the existence of, for example, non-binary people with dyslexia. On the other hand, Gheno (2022) does acknowledge the potential impact on accessibility, with speech synthesisers not currently handling gender-inclusive characters well, which can cause problems for the blind and visually impaired.

Portuguese: The Portuguese translation team consists of six translators, all from Brazil (Portugal is a 'region of interest' for the IQA, but has no NGB yet). The team leader wishes to introduce gender-inclusive language in official IQA translations in the future, but has decided against it at the moment. The main reason for taking a cautious approach is the fact that gender-inclusive language is not actively being used in Brazil yet, not even by the LGBTQIA+ community, and that there is a strong anti-trans agenda in media and politics. The translation team is taking a year to work on a variety of resources for their community and to explore attitudes towards gender-inclusive language and will introduce this gender-inclusive language in IQA translations from next year onwards. The team has developed referee tests specific for their community, using gender-inclusive language, and is conducting a survey asking referees about their impressions, the comprehension and readability of the questions and related rulebook excerpts. They are also developing additional referee resources (videos and rulebook comprehension questions) using gender-inclusive writing. Preliminary findings from their survey seem to indicate that people find the gender-inclusive writing hard to understand at first, but get used to it after a while. However, people with dyslexia or ADHD seem to find it the hardest to use and understand.

Recent research indeed seems to suggest that there is no commonly accepted gender-inclusive strategy for Portuguese, with Pinheiro (2020) arguing that any suggested changes to the morphosyntactic and semantic level of the Portuguese language are met with a lot of resistance in Brazil, although they also claim that society is becoming more aware of the idea of non-binary gender identities. Comparing a variety of suggested strategies (the use of marked feminine, presenting feminine and masculine forms, using new word endings such as -x, -@, or -e), Schwindt (2020) claims that changes to the language are possible, provided they come with a sufficient degree of spontaneity and naturalness (i.e., taking into account the phonological, morphological, syntactic and semantic restrictions of the language). Of the suggested word endings, the '-e' seems the most likely to succeed, given that it can be pronounced (in contrast with -x and -@, which additionally pose problems for screen readers) and that it already has a morphological role in the language (Schwindt, 2020).

Spanish: The size of the Spanish translation team fluctuates greatly. At the time of writing it consisted of four translators. The decision to use inclusive language was driven by the team leader, inspired by the IQA's values of inclusivity. There was a vote in the translators' chat (there were more than four translators on the team at the time of the vote), where they unanimously agreed to use this strategy. The NGBs (plural, as Spanish is spoken in European as well as Latin American NGBs) were not consulted, as the team leader feared this would lead to unnecessary debate. The team leader is aware of a variety of suggested strategies for Spanish inclusive writing currently in use in practice:

- Using '–x' to replace gender markings (e.g., 'lxs árbitrxs'). Pro: seen in Latin-American texts, con: very uncommon in Spain (particularly Galicia), hard to pronounce.

- Duplication, using both masculine and feminine versions of a word if possible (e.g., 'Los árbitros y las árbitras'). Pro: used in official documents and quite widespread, con: text becomes longer and potentially harder to read, risk of exacerbating genderization of gender neutral words.
- Avoidance, by using collective or gender neutral words (e.g., 'el equipo de árbitros' instead of 'los árbitros'). Pro: as unmarked as possible, also used in official documents, con: not always possible, avoiding gendered words can lead to 'pedantic' phrasing.
- Using '-e' to replace gender markings (e.g., 'les árbitres'). Pro: easy to use, economic, includes people of all genders, con: actively opposed, particularly by right-wing people.

The last two strategies are the strategies currently in use at the IQA. The collective or gender neutral words strategy is the team leader's preferred strategy. They consider the '-e' strategy to be the most radical "as it is the productive one, the one that can actually work as one can pronounce it and use it in both conversation and texts". While the strategy is increasingly being used by leftist minorities, it is often ridiculed or even actively opposed. Arguments against the use of gender-inclusive language are that it is supposedly harder to read, and that the Real Academia Española de la Lengua (a very prescriptivist language organisation) is against it as well. To learn more about the subject, the team leader follows the work by Ártemis López[2], a PhD researcher working on non-binary language in Spanish.

Studying the perception of translators towards gender-inclusive language in Chile, Uriarte Castro (2022) indeed found that translators generally prefer to use less disruptive forms of inclusive language, although there is a difference between older translators (finding adherence to the language's norms most important, worrying about the readability of a text) and younger translators (finding it important to respect people's gender identities). Recent research on non-binary language in Spanish suggests that the '-x' and '-e' strategies are not harder to read than generic masculine (-o) variants and that 'generic' masculine actually causes male bias, which the non-binary strategies avoid (Stetie & Zunino, 2022). With regards to preference, the '-e' strategy indeed seems to be the most preferred at the moment (Slemp, 2020; Hiers 2022).

3.2 Similarities and differences across languages

All translation team leaders seem to agree that gender-inclusive language is important to represent the IQA values of gender-inclusivity, although the degree to which this is already actively implemented varies across languages. While Catalan, French, German, and Spanish translators actively use gender-inclusive language to some degree for all documents, Italian translators avoid it for content chapters of the rulebook, and Portuguese translators are gradually moving towards more gender-inclusive language, giving the community time to get acquainted with the new strategy before officially putting it to use.

The main strategies currently in use are the following:

- Indirect Non-binary Language (avoiding gender by using collective or generic words): Catalan, Spanish
- Direct Non-binary Language:
    - Using typographical characters to explicitly include non-binary individuals: French, German
    - Using gender-inclusive morphemes: Italian, Spanish

There are some interesting differences with regards to the role of the NGBs in the decision-making process. While French, German, and Portuguese translation teams closely consulted their NGBs, the Spanish team leader considers the NGBs opinion of secondary importance to the IQA's values, and the Catalan NGB often followed the lead of the IQA translators.

Particularly striking is the fact that many team leaders explicitly refer to academic research on the subject, or the attitudes towards the language in their communities and countries. Even in situations where gender-inclusive language is not used (yet), this seems to be a very conscious decision.

4 Translator awareness and attitude

To get a better understanding of how translators perceive gender-inclusive language at the IQA, I conducted a survey using Google Forms. The survey consisted of three main parts:

- **Personal background**, asking participants about their language, gender, education or professional background, and how important the gender-inclusivity of the sport was for them to join as a player or as a volunteer.
- **Gender-inclusive language strategy**, a more general section asking about participants'

[2] https://www.queerterpreter.com/

awareness of gender-inclusive language strategies in use for their language, how important it is to them, what they think of the readability, and what the general attitude towards it is in their countries.

- **Gender-inclusive language at the IQA**, asking how important they feel this is, how important potential factors are when deciding which strategy to use, how aware they themselves are of those potentially relevant factors, how they feel about the strategy currently in use in their team.

The form was shared with translators via the IQA Slack workspace and e-mail. The total number of translators invited to participate was 27 (19 official IQA translators on Slack and an additional 8 community translators currently working on IQA translation projects). It must be noted that activity fluctuates greatly among translators, as these are unpaid volunteer positions, and many translators also volunteer within their own communities (either for local teams or within their NGBs), making some people less likely to regularly check the IQA Slack or e-mails.

4.1 Personal background

The survey was filled out by 11 translators (1 Catalan, 1 French, 2 Portuguese, 3 Spanish, and 4 German). There were 2 non-binary, 5 female, and 4 male participants.

Only one translator indicated they have a translation background, and three indicated that they have language or linguistics related backgrounds. Two indicated they have a background in gender studies, although two more clarified in the comments that gender does play a significant role in their lives (being trans or having obtained a degree in sociology with a strong gender perspective). Most translators (9) are currently also players, with one translator indicating they used to play but now only volunteer, and one only volunteering and having no intention of playing the sport.

As can be seen in Figures 1 & 2, for at least half of the translators, the gender-inclusive element of the sport was important or very important to join either as a player or a volunteer, with a higher number of participants indicating that it was not at all important for them to join as a volunteer compared to the numbers for joining as a player. For female or non-binary translators, the element of inclusivity seems to be more important in both cases than for male translators.

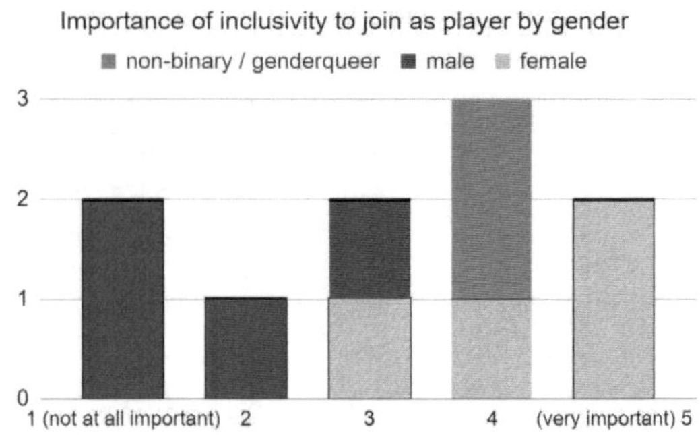

Figure 1: Importance of gender-inclusivity to join as a player by gender (1 = 'Not at all important, I would have joined even if it hadn't been inclusive'; 5 = 'Very important, I wouldn't have joined if it wasn't inclusive')

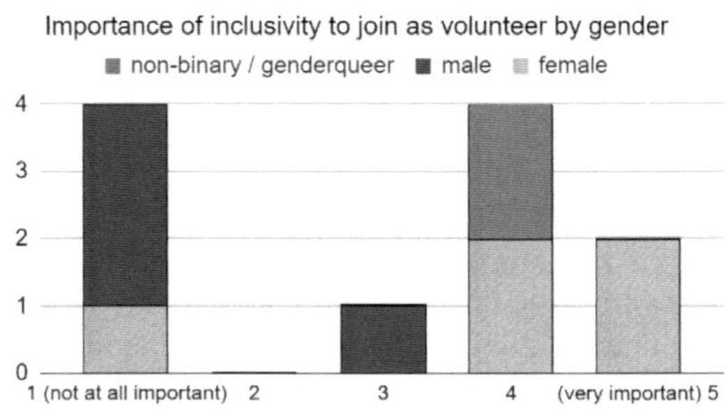

Figure 2: Importance of gender-inclusivity to join as a volunteer by gender (1 = 'Not at all important, I would have joined even if it hadn't been inclusive'; 5 = 'Very important, I wouldn't have joined if it wasn't inclusive')

4.2 Gender-inclusive language strategies

Five of the translators find it very important to see gender-inclusive writing in a text, with none of the translators indicating they don't find it important at all (Figure 3). Perhaps somewhat surprisingly, the trend in relation to gender seems different from that in Figures 1 & 2, with female and non-binary translators finding it somewhat less important to see gender-inclusive writing than male translators do[3].

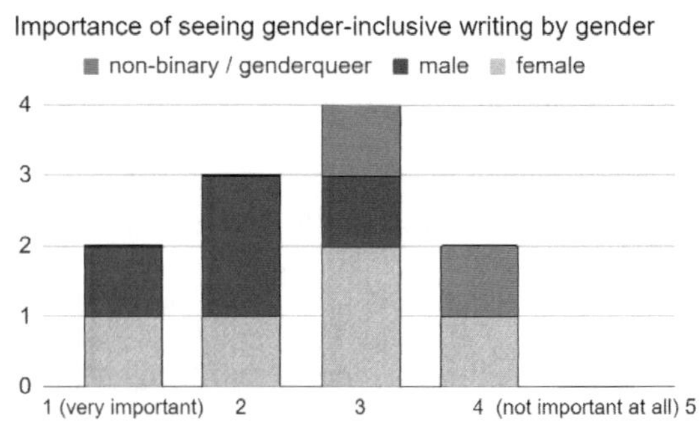

Figure 3: Importance of seeing gender-inclusive writing (1 = 'Very important'; 5 = 'Not important at all')

[3] It is of course always possible that respondents misinterpreted the values (in the first two questions, 1 was 'not at all important' and 5 was 'very important, whereas those labels were flipped for this question).

In the comments, translators clarified that it depends on the context and type of text, and the tradeoff between inclusivity and readability. The next question asked how readable participants found texts written in gender-inclusive language compared to non-inclusive writing. Five of the participants seem to find both equally readable (see Figure 4), whereas most other participants find inclusive writing harder to read. Only one person indicated that they found it much easier to read.

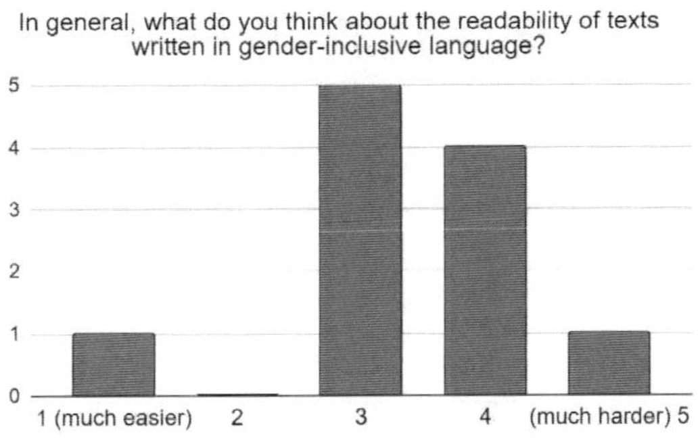

Figure 4: Readability (1 = 'I find gender-inclusive writing much easier to read than non-inclusive writing.'; 5 = 'I find gender-inclusive writing much harder to read than non-inclusive writing.')

In the comments, translators clarified that it really depends on the language and the type of gender-inclusive writing. English was seen as very readable compared to German and Portuguese, and generic words (e.g. 'people') were seen as easier to read than typographical strategies or new gender-inclusive morphemes. One translator also indicated that it is a matter of getting used to it.

Most translators (8) were already aware about gender-inclusive writing strategies for their language before joining the IQA. Based on the answers in the comments, translators know about the following strategies for their language (number of translators who mention this strategy in brackets):

- Indirect Non-binary Language: avoiding gender by using collective or generic words (7)
- Direct Non-binary Language:
  - Using typographical characters (5)
  - Using gender-inclusive morphemes and/or pronouns (4)
- Others:
  - Alternating between male/female forms (2)
  - Feminine gender only (1)

When asked about their favorite strategy, six out of seven translators write that they prefer the avoidance strategy, as it can be used and read relatively easily. Or as one translator explained it: "Sometimes it is important to show that inclusion does not have to be controversial, it can be something VERY natural". Some translators do remark that this strategy is not always possible, and that it needs to be combined with others.

In general, translators perceive the attitudes towards gender-inclusive writing in their language as somewhat more negative (see Figure 5), with none of the translators going for the 'mostly positive' option.

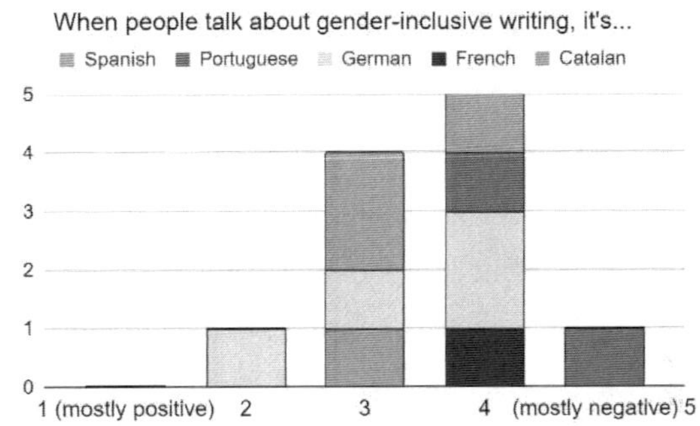

Figure 5: In general (not specific to the IQA context), what describes the situation for your language best? (1 = 'When people talk about gender-inclusive writing, it's mostly positive'; 5 = 'When people talk about gender-inclusive writing, it's mostly negative')

In the comments, translators explain that it depends on the people, with younger people, women, and people from the LGBTQIA+ and/or the quadball community much more likely to be positive towards this kind of language. The 'average person' is described as not liking language change, and criticizing any gender-inclusive writing forms that feel too hard to read.

4.3 Gender-inclusive translation at the IQA

When it comes to the use of gender-inclusive language by the IQA translation team, most translators seem to agree that gender-inclusive language should always (7) or often (2) be used (see Figure 6). There is a fairly even spread among the female translators, whereas the non-binary and male translators mostly go for the 'always' option.

The main reasons listed by the translators relate to gender-inclusivity being a core value of the sport, and the IQA needing to be at the forefront of this change. Translators who did not choose 'always' clarify that for them it depends on the type of text and the kind of language, and that readability should always be taken into account, particularly for the rulebook and referee tests. When given a list of potential factors that should be taken into account when determining a translation strategy (Figure 7), most translators indeed indicate that 'readability' is very (8) or even extremely (2) important.

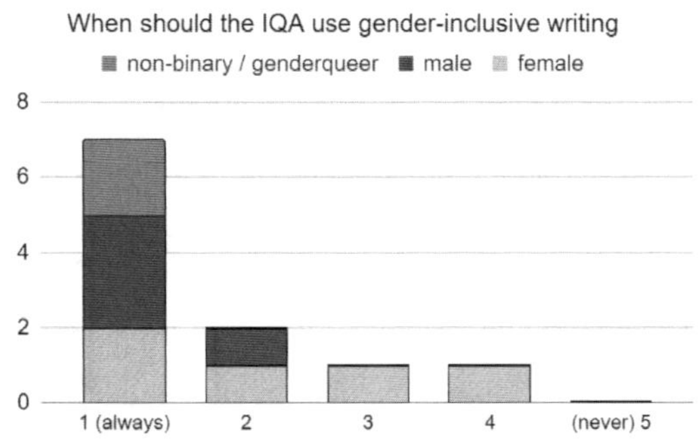

Figure 6: How do you personally feel about gender-inclusive writing in the context of IQA translations? (1 = 'The IQA should always use gender-inclusive writing in translation.'; 5 = 'The IQA should never use gender-inclusive writing in translation.')

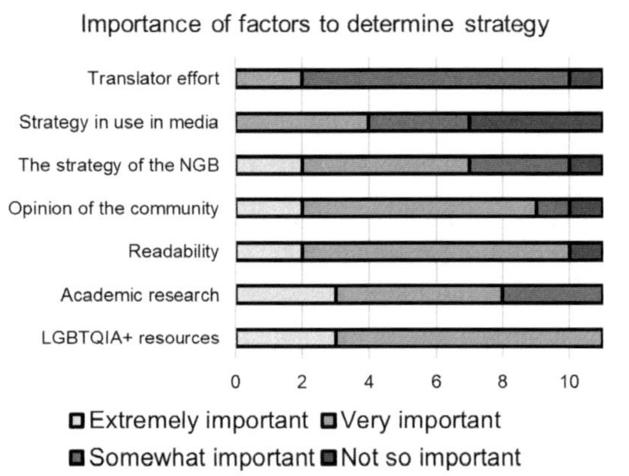

Figure 7: Importance of factors to determine gender-inclusive translation strategies ('Not at all important' was never chosen by any translator).

Other important factors according to the translators are LGBTQIA+ resources (3 'extremely', 8 'very), academic research (3 'extremely', 5 'very'), the opinion of the IQA community (2 'extremely', 7 'very'), and the strategy of the NGB to a lesser degree (2 'extremely', 5 'very', but also 3 'somewhat' and 1 'not so'). The strategy used by media or in official documentation and the effort for the translator are seen as less important, with more than half of the translators choosing 'somewhat important' and 'not so important' and none of the translators selecting 'extremely important'. Translators were also challenged to only choose one factor as 'the most important' one, and chose the following (number of translators who chose the option between brackets):

- The readability of the text (3): Those advocating for readability clarify that a text loses its purpose if it cannot be understood. One participant also explains that readers can be taught to understand gender-inclusive writing, for example by providing guides explaining the choices made in their native language.
- Academic research (2) and LGBTQIA+ resources (1): Presented together as one translator wrote that academic research also takes the LGBTQIA+ perspective into account.
- The opinion of the community (2): Translators explain that the work the IQA does needs to serve the community, and the members of the community are the ones that need to understand the resources the IQA provides.

The other three participants indicated 'something else', with two of them also referring to the importance of the community in their clarification, mentioning that the strategy should help the community and that it should include everyone in the community (particularly including non-binary individuals). The third person said it is always a compromise.

When asked about their personal awareness of certain factors (the opinion of the community, LGBTQIA+ resources, academic research, and the strategy of the NGB), the majority (6-8) of respondents seems to be aware of them, with most translators being aware of the strategies currently in use by their NGB (see Figure 8).

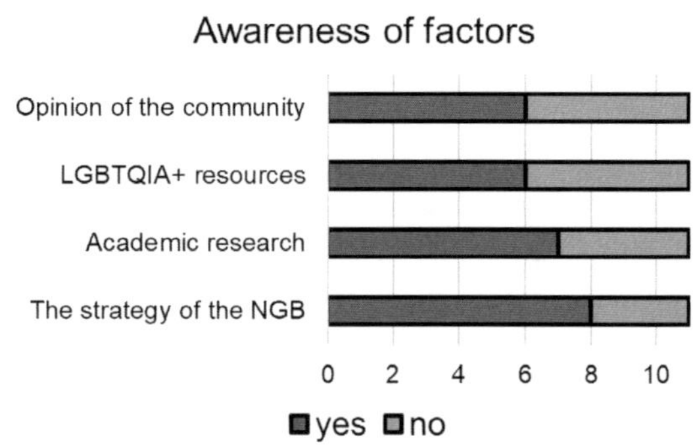

Figure 8: Translator awareness of factors to determine gender-inclusive translation strategies.

Of the seven people that indicated that they are aware of academic research on gender-inclusive writing for their language, there are four that have a background in either translation, linguistics, or gender studies, and three without such a background. Before joining the IQA, six translators didn't use gender-inclusive writing in their language, whereas five did.

When asked whether translators are aware of the strategy currently in use in their team, there does seem to be a little confusion. In the German team, there was one translator who thought the asterisk was still being used, and one who indicated that only female forms were being used. For Spanish, one of the translators indicated they didn't know whether or not gender-inclusive writing was being used.

Of the eight translators in teams that already use gender-inclusive writing strategies (and are aware of them), six are mostly happy about the strategy currently in use, although some add that it is "the best *for now*" [emphasis mine]. There seems to be a tension between readability/inclusivity, with on the one hand a need to make female players more visible (one translator indicated that the '-e' strategy in Spanish feels like it's making females invisible, another joked that it would be nice to release a text where everyone is gendered female), and on the other to make sure players of all genders are included: "It doesn't really represent all genders now, but the readability has improved a lot."

When asked how hard it was to translate using gender-inclusive strategies, most translators (6) indicated that it was just as easy/hard to do as using non-inclusive writing for their language, and five indicated that it was harder to do (selecting 4 on a Likert scale from 1-5 with 1 being 'much easier than using non-inclusive writing for my language, and 5 being 'much harder than using non-inclusive writing for my language'). Reasons why it is seen as harder is because there is more typing or thinking, it needs more rereading (particularly in grammatically complex sentences), and because a lot of gender-inclusive terms and strategy are new to people. On the other hand, translators in both groups indicate that it does get easier as they get used to it.

5 Discussion

The IQA translation teams have a clear understanding of the importance of gender-inclusive language strategies and are very aware of the community they translate for (both the quadball and the broader LGBTQIA+ community), which follows the recommendations of Attig (2022). The fact that strategies change as new research becomes available, or even when the translation team leader changes confirms the findings by Lardelli and Gromann (2023) that there is no 'one-size-fits-all' solution to determining gender-inclusive translation strategies.

At the IQA, the strategies are different for each language, and sometimes even change depending on the context. This can be seen most clearly in some teams' decision to change their strategy when translating the referee tests. These tests are taken under strict time limits, and there is a concern that gender-inclusive language forms might be harder to read. On the other hand, recent research suggests that this might not be the case in practice (Friedrich et al., 2021; Girard et al., 2021; Liénardy et al., 2023; Stetie & Zunino, 2022). Team leaders explicitly mention the potential negative influence on people with dyslexia, ADHD, or learning disabilities. To the best of my knowledge, this effect has not been tested in practice, making it a potentially fruitful avenue for future research. Another aspect of gender-inclusive writing where the inclusion of one group might happen at the cost of the inclusion of another is in the visibility of women. While there is some evidence that gender-inclusive strategies actually improve the visibility of women compared to the generic masculine (Liénardy et al., 2023; Stetie & Zunino, 2022; Tibblin et al., 2023), this may not be true for all languages or all strategies (e.g. Robustelli, 2021). Going forward, it will be crucial to evaluate the impact of different strategies from an intersectional point of view.

Because of the variability and continuously evolving strategies, translation technology at the IQA is currently limited to the use of translation memories and glossaries within Matecat (Federico et al., 2014) to ensure consistency in projects with more than one translator. Machine translation is not seen as a viable solution at this point as "machine translation cannot adapt to rapidly-evolving non-binary language" (Dev et al., 2021) and "one generally acceptable and widely applicable solution does not and could not exist" (Lardelli & Gromann, 2023). I am aware of some of the recent suggestions in this field (Piergentili et al., 2023) and will continue to follow these evolutions.

6 Conclusion & future work

As gender-inclusivity is one of the core values of quadball, this exploratory study set out to determine how gender-inclusivity is currently implemented by the different IQA translation teams, by means of input from translation team leaders and a survey conducted among the IQA translators.

Input from team leaders showed that each language has a different strategy, with languages like Portuguese and Italian taking a more cautious approach but willing to increase the use of gender-inclusive language in the future, Catalan preferring an Indirect Non-binary Language approach, and French, German, and Spanish opting for Direct Non-binary Language approaches. Factors that are taken into account are the gender-inclusive element of the sport, awareness of community needs, input from LGBTQIA+ communities and linguistic research.

Translators agree that gender-inclusive language should be used by the IQA, and seem to find LGBTQIA+ resources, academic research, the opinion of the community and the readability of a text the most important factors to determine a strategy. The argument of 'readability' occurs frequently, among team leaders and translators alike, although actual empirical research on readability, particularly for people with learning disabilities, is currently scarce to nonexistent.

Overall, it is clear from the feedback that the gender-inclusive language strategies are not set in stone, and that team leaders and translators are open to changing the strategy as new information becomes available. Given the fact that gender-inclusive language is constantly evolving and that translators indicate that they get used to reading and writing it as they do it more, my goal is to repeat this survey every (other) year, to eventually get a diachronic overview of the evolution in the respective IQA communities. In a next phase, I hope to expand the present survey with a survey among NGB board members and players, to explore the attitudes in the community at large. Particularly interesting would be a comparison of referee tests using different language strategies, to empirically verify whether or not a gender-inclusive strategy is indeed harder to read (with regards to speed and comprehension).

Disclaimers

The author is Assistant Professor at Ghent University and volunteers as Translation Manager at the IQA. They speak English and Dutch (and have notions of French and German), which necessarily reduces the body of potentially relevant work they have access to (when it comes to gender-inclusive language strategies, researchers often work in their respective language). Sources in other languages were translated with the help of Google Translate and are presented to the best of the author's ability. At the time of writing, the IQA was undergoing a name change. The new name has been used here, to future-proof the text.

References

Académie française. (7 May 2021). Lettre ouverte sur l'écriture inclusive. Retrieved via https://www.academie-francaise.fr/actualites/lettre-ouverte-sur-lecriture-inclusive

Attig, R. (2022). A call for community-informed translation: Respecting Queer self-determination across linguistic lines. *Translation and Interpreting Studies*.

Bukof (Bundeskonferenz der Frauen- und Gleichstellungsbeauftragten an Hochschulen). (2022). *Doppelpunkt oder Sternchen? Zur Frage der Barrierearmut einer gendersensiblen Sprache*. Retrieved via https://bukof.de/wp-content/uploads/22-06-07-bukof-Stellungnahme-Doppelpunkt-oder-Sternchen-1.pdf

Comandini, G. (2021). Salve a tuttə, tutt*, tuttu, tuttx e tutt@: l'uso delle strategie di neutralizzazione di genere nella comunità queer online.: Indagine su un corpus di italiano scritto informale sul web. *Testo e Senso, 23*, 43-64.

D'Achille, P. (2021). Un asterisco sul genere. *Consulenza linguistica*.

De Santis, C. (2022), L'emancipazione grammaticale non passa per una e rovesciata, in *Treccani Scritto e parlato, 9 febbraio*. Retrieved via https://www.treccani.it/magazine/lingua_italiana/articoli/scritto_e_parlato/Schwa.html

Dev, S., Monajatipoor, M., Ovalle, A., Subramonian, A., Phillips, J. M., & Chang, K. W. (2021). Harms of gender exclusivity and challenges in non-binary representation in language technologies. *arXiv preprint arXiv:2108.12084*.

Duarte, J. (2022). *Catalan*. Gender in Language Project. www.genderinlanguage.com/catalan

Federico, M., Bertoldi, N., Cettolo, M., Negri, M., Turchi, M., Trombetti, M., ... & Germann, U. (2014, August). The MateCat tool. In *COLING (Demos)* (pp. 129-132).

Friedrich, M. C., Drößler, V., Oberlehberg, N., & Heise, E. (2021). The influence of the gender asterisk ("Gendersternchen") on comprehensibility and interest. *Frontiers in psychology, 12*, 760062.

Gheno, V. (2022). Questione di privilegi: come il linguaggio ampio può contribuire ad ampliare gli orizzonti mentali. *AG About Gender-International Journal of Gender Studies, 11*(21), 388-406.

Girard, G., Foucambert, D., & Le Mené, M. (2021). Lisibilité de l'écriture inclusive: apports des techniques d'oculométrie.

Hiers, J. E. (2022). *Spanish Teacher Attitudes toward Gender-Neutral Spanish Forms*. Master's thesis, The University of North Carolina at Chapel Hill.

Hord, Levi C. R. (2016). Bucking the Linguistic Binary: Gender Neutral Language in English, Swedish, French, and German, *Western Papers in Linguistics / Cahiers linguistiques de Wester, 3*(1), Article 4.

IQA Rulebook 2022. Via https://iqasport.org/about/documents-and-policies

Junyent, M. C. (2021). Som dones, som lingüistes, som moltes i diem prou. *Eumo Editorial. Vic*.

Koeser, S., Kuhn, E. A., & Sczesny, S. (2015). Just reading? How gender-fair language triggers readers' use of gender-fair forms. *Journal of Language and Social Psychology, 34*(3), 343-357.

Kosnick, K. (2019). The everyday poetics of gender-inclusive French: strategies for navigating the linguistic landscape. *Modern & Contemporary France, 27*(2), 147-161.

Lardelli, M., & Gromann, D. (2023). Gender-fair (machine) translation. In *Proceedings of the New Trends in Translation and Technology Conference - NeTTT 2022*, 166–177.

Liénardy, C., Tibblin, J., Gygax, P., & Simon, A. C. (2023). Écriture inclusive, lisibilité textuelle et représentations mentales. *Discours*.

López, Á. (2022). Trans (de) letion: Audiovisual translations of gender identities for mainstream audiences. *Journal of Language and Sexuality*, *11*(2), 217-239.

Manesse, D. (2022). Contre l'écriture inclusive. *Travail, genre et sociétés, 47*(1), 169-172.

Piergentili, A., Fucci, D., Savoldi, B., Bentivogli, L., & Negri, M. (2023). From Inclusive Language to Gender-Neutral Machine Translation. *arXiv preprint arXiv:2301.10075.*

Pinheiro, L. R. R. (2020). Linguagem neutra: a reestruturação do gênero no Português brasileiro frente às mudanças sociais.

Robustelli, C. (2021). Lo schwa? Una toppa peggiore del buco. *Micromega.* https://www. micromega. net/schwa-problemi-limiti-cecilia-robustelli

Schwindt, L. C. (2020). Sobre gênero neutro em português brasileiro e os limites do sistema linguístico. *Revista da Abralin, 19*(1), 1–23.

Sczesny, S., Formanowicz, M., & Moser, F. (2016). Can gender-fair language reduce gender stereotyping and discrimination?. *Frontiers in psychology*, 25.

Slemp, K. (2020). *Latino, Latina, Latin@, Latine, and Latinx: gender inclusive oral expression in Spanish.* Electronic Thesis and Dissertation Repository. 7297. https://ir.lib.uwo.ca/etd/7297

Stahlberg, D., Braun, F., Irmen, L., and Sczesny, S. (2007). "Representation of the sexes in language," in *Social Communication. A Volume in the Series Frontiers of Social Psychology*, ed. K. Fiedler (New York, NY: Psychology Press), 163–187

Stetie, N. A., & Zunino, G. M. (2022). Non-binary language in Spanish? Comprehension of non-binary morphological forms: a psycholinguistic study. *Glossa: a journal of general linguistics*, *7*(1), 1-38.

Tibblin, J., van de Weijer, J., Granfeldt, J., & Gygax, P. (2023). There are more women in joggeur· euses than in joggeurs: On the effects of gender-fair forms on perceived gender ratios in French role nouns. *Journal of French Language Studies*, *33*(1), 28-51.

Uriarte Castro, C. (2022). Lenguaje inclusivo no sexista en traducción: perspectivas de traductores y traductoras profesionales.

Participatory Research as a Path to Community-Informed, Gender-Fair Machine Translation

Dagmar Gromann[1], **Manuel Lardelli**[2], **Katta Spiel**[3], **Sabrina Burtscher**[3], **Lukas Daniel Klausner**[4], **Arthur Mettinger**[5], **Igor Miladinovic**[5], **Sigrid Schefer-Wenzl**[5], **Daniela Duh**[5], and **Katharina Bühn**[5]

[1]University of Vienna, Austria, {name.surname}@univie.ac.at
[2]University of Graz, Austria, {name.surname}@uni-graz.at
[3]TU Wien, Austria, {name.surname}@tuwien.ac.at
[4]St. Pölten University of Applied Sciences, Austria, mail@l17r.eu
[5]FH Campus Wien University of Applied Sciences
{name.surname}@fh-campuswien.ac.at

Abstract

Recent years have seen a strongly increased visibility of non-binary people in public discourse. Accordingly, considerations of gender-fair language go beyond a binary conception of male/female. However, language technology, especially machine translation (MT), still suffers from binary gender bias. Proposing a solution for gender-fair MT beyond the binary from a purely technological perspective might fall short to accommodate different target user groups and in the worst case might lead to misgendering. To address this challenge, we propose a method and case study building on participatory action research to include experiential experts, i.e., queer and non-binary people, translators, and MT experts, in the MT design process. The case study focuses on German, where central findings are the importance of context dependency to avoid identity invalidation and a desire for customizable MT solutions.

1 Introduction

With an increased visibility of non-binary people in public discourse, gender-fair language strategies to go beyond a binary conception of male/female have been proposed. Gender-fair language subsumes gender-inclusive, i.e., linguistically including all gender identities, and gender-neutral, i.e., removing all gender references, strategies. Practically applying gender-fair language across grammatically different languages is challenging for human and machine translation. In human gender-fair translation, substantial errors can be observed (Lardelli and Gromann, Forthcoming; Attig, 2022). In MT, the "masculine default" might have been mitigated with strategies to debias MT, however, generally with a binary focus (Savoldi et al., 2021) and not linguistically acknowledging existing gender identities with few exceptions (Saunders and Byrne, 2020; Piergentili et al., 2023). Savoldi et al. (2021) call for research beyond NLP and its "narrow, problem-solving oriented approach" to advance the field and Attig (2022) proposes to include queer and non-binary people in a community-informed translation process.

The proposed case study builds on the notion that gender-fair (machine) translation requires an early community involvement. The word "machine" is at times placed in brackets since there was a common consensus that first gender-fair translation strategies are required to facilitate gender-fair MT. To this end, ten researchers in Austria organized a three-day workshop with in total 21 participants from three groups of stakeholders, i.e., queer and non-binary people, professional translators, and MT experts, to reflect on their experiences, desires, and concerns regarding MT. Furthermore, we seek to provide a method that emphasizes the importance of human value, similar to the Diverse Voices method (Young et al., 2019), and includes marginalized groups in technology design, i.e., with participatory design (Spiel et al., 2020). In the proposed method, Participatory Action Research (PAR) is utilized to design a set of activities to identify problems, desires, strategies, and proposed adaptations to the MT design process, as depicted in Fig. 1.

Eva Vanmassenhove, Beatrive Savoldi, Luisa Bentivogli, Joke Daems & Janiça Hackenbuchner
Proceedings of the 1st Workshop on Gender-Inclusive Translation Technologies, p. 49–59
Tampere, Finland, June 2023.

In MT, it has been proposed to solve the issue by focusing on gender-neutral strategies (Piergentili et al., 2023), which, however, cannot be applied to all contexts, especially not without information loss, and might not be the strategy preferred by all MT users. In fact, findings from this workshop challenge the current MT paradigm of one input equals one output and reveal strong preferences for a customizable solutions that allow users to select their preferred strategy and make context-informed suggestions. To the best of our knowledge, this is the first community-informed workshop on gender-fair (machine) translation with the explicit purpose to include human value and marginalized groups in the technology design process. In this paper, we describe the activities themselves, their practical implementation as a workshop with three groups of stakeholders, and a potential blueprint of the activities to develop similar workshops for other languages and communities.

2 Preliminaries

To provide a theoretical basis for the following discussion, we first briefly explain the discourse on gender and language, and PAR as well as stakeholder selection taken from value-sensitive design.

2.1 Gender and Language

The term gender involves biological aspects, i.e., functionality of brains, production of hormones, as well as psychological, i.e., the way people identify, experience, think about gender, and social aspects, i.e., how gender is enacted in a particular context (Barker and Iantaffi, 2019). Gender identities are self-determined and not assigned (Zimman, 2019) and beyond the male/female dichotomy range from agender, genderfluid to non-binary or pangender among many others (Richards et al., 2016). Gender identities are crucial in daily lives since they are used as a criterion to regulate access to services and goods (Fae, 2016) as well as public spaces, such as restrooms (van Anders et al., 2017).

Structurally, natural languages have been categorized into grammatical gender, notional gender, and genderless languages (Stahlberg et al., 2007; Savoldi et al., 2021). In grammatical gender languages, nouns, adjectives, pronouns, and determiners are gender-inflected. In notional gender languages, such as English, lexical gender, such as *boy* and *girl*, derivational nouns, such as *waiter* and *waitress*, and pronouns are gender-specific. In genderless languages, such as Finnish, mostly references to kinship are gendered, e.g. *sister* and *brother*. Gender is not only a matter of grammatical gender, but also a social construct and can emerge in the way language is used, which reflects assumptions and norms on gender identity.

Gender-Fair German Inspired by Sczesny et al. (2016), we subsume gender-inclusive and gender-neutral strategies as gender-fair language. Gender-inclusive strategies, which seek to make all genders visible, can be of two different types: (1) typographical characters (*, :, _) to separate male from female forms and include all genders, e.g. *Leser*innen* (reader) and *sie*er* (she*he) (Hornscheidt and Sammla, 2021); (2) new gender systems, such as the SYLVAIN system (de Sylvain and Balzer, 2008), that introduce a fourth grammatical gender in addition to masculine, feminine and neuter, e.g. *Lesernin* (reader). Gender-neutral strategies can vary, ranging from the use of typographical characters to remove any gender endings, such as *Les**, and rewording to the introduction of neutral endings and pronouns, e.g. *Lesens* and *ens* (Hornscheidt and Sammla, 2021).

Impact of Gender Bias Bias in language technology can be defined as systems that "*systematically* and *unfairly discriminate* against certain individuals or groups of individuals in favour of others" (Friedman and Nissenbaum, 1996). Bias in the training data leads to MT systems with biased predictions, e.g. sampling non-random subsets of data. The main impact of gender bias is the harm that can be produced by a biased system. Crawford (2017) differentiates between allocational and representational harms. The former refer to the allocation or withholding of opportunities or resources to certain groups. The latter refer to lessening or omitting the representation of specific groups and their identity. Not recognizing the existence of gender beyond the binary can imply the harm of disregarding the language used by these communities (Savoldi et al., 2021). Misgendering, the assignment of a wrong gender to a person, should be added to the list, which can lead to emotional pain and a feeling of identity invalidation (Zimman, 2019). Finally, stereotyping refers to propagating negative generalizations of a social group (Savoldi et al., 2021).

2.2 Participatory Action Research

Participatory Action Research (PAR) is a highly community-led approach that allows for different stances that, when combined, deliver a more vibrant description of agendas and contexts of use than researchers' perspectives could provide on their own (Hayes, 2011). With action research as a methodological base, this method is committed to have a positive transformative impact on the individuals' lives as well as further representatives of the associated communities. Concretely, this means also to actively facilitate negotiation between different stakeholder groups and their potentially contradicting needs and desires.

A typical PAR process consists of alternating action and reflection phases (Kindon et al., 2007), where action focuses on building relationships and performing collaborative activities and reflections focus on research design/process, ethics, knowledge and accountability as well as towards the end on how well the collaboration has worked and further steps that are required. Typical activities include dialog, storytelling, and collective action that with their hands-on nature are particularly adequate for work with marginalized or vulnerable people since they allow participants to generate information and share knowledge on their own terms using their own language (Kindon et al., 2007).

2.3 Value Sensitive Design

Value Sensitive Design (VSD) seeks to account for human values in technology design, where values substantially depend on the interests and desires of human beings within a specific context (Friedman et al., 2013). VSD considers direct and indirect stakeholders, where the former are those that directly interact with the technology and the latter are those impacted by the technology, even if potentially never touching the technology itself. Stakeholders may span more than one role in a design process, e.g. translator and non-binary in our case study. VSD can further help in deciding on which stakeholder groups to prioritize, where we follow Young et al. (2019) in prioritizing transparency over specific ethical or other concerns. We seek to include these groups that impact and are most likely impacted by the technology, but who have yet been underrepresented in previous research, i.e., queer and non-binary people.

3 Objective

In our initial endeavors to develop a gender-fair MT model, we quickly realized that we not only lack training datasets but sufficient knowledge to decide on a gender-fair strategy for German. Thus, our objective in organizing a workshop was to bring together three communities to jointly discuss considerations and implications that should be taken into account in designing gender-fair MT solutions.

Queer and non-binary people represent indirect stakeholders in the sense that their interaction with MT in the past or future is neither a given nor a requirement. Nevertheless, this group is substantially impacted by gender-fair language use or the lack thereof. The active use of gender-inclusive or gender-neutral strategies in MT could positively affect the visibility of gender diversity, since its use is widespread and users are frequently not even aware of consuming MT outputs (Martindale and Carpuat, 2018).

Professional translators are both direct and indirect stakeholders. In spite of some resistance (Cadwell et al., 2018), MT is increasingly integrated into translation pipelines (Way, 2020), which makes translators direct stakeholders. On the other hand, as providers of translations for training MT models, they are indirect stakeholders who impact the technology. While translators at times might have been included in post-editing or MT evaluation studies, the two groups above have to the best of our knowledge not been included in the MT design and development process.

Finally, we decided to select MT developers/researchers as a stakeholder group to gather insights into the feasibility of ideas devised in group discussions and include their perspective on this topic in the cross-community exchange. To reach stakeholders, it is vital to include facilitators who are trustworthy to the respective communities, in particular in case of sensitive topics, and who can rely on personal networks and contacts for invitations of stakeholders. Furthermore, such facilitators, in our case as part of the research team, need to actively help shape the plan in an appropriate and acceptable manner for participants, moderate the workshop, and intervene in group discussions if stagnation or conflicts arise.

In terms of method, our objective was to encourage participants to share their experiences, desires, and concerns as well as informed critique on existing gender-fair (machine) translation strategies and requirements. Participatory Action Research (PAR) is designed to elicit and generate situated knowledge that provides insights beyond a unique case study and ensures an interactive, motivating design. Thus, the design of our activities follows the PAR principles and cycles.

4 Participatory Workshop Activities

The workshop plan was designed to alternate interactive sessions in small groups and plenary discussions on each of the five main topics and stages depicted in Fig. 1. Activities in small groups deliberately alternated between groups constituted by members of the same stakeholder group (community-internal) and groups with members of each stakeholder group (cross-community). Each interactive group activity was planned for approx. one hour and accompanied by written instructions, followed by approx. 30 minutes of presentation of results and plenary discussion. At the end of each day, a joint summary of major topics and findings was to be prepared in plenary session, including interactive quizzes and word clouds on Mentimeter.

4.1 Warm-Up Phase

For the registration, voluntary colored stickers to indicate a) the stakeholder group and b) the pronouns of participants were foreseen. As an ice-breaker, a first sociometric introduction asked participants to position themselves along different axes of the room for a number of off-topic, e.g. means of transportation to arrive at the workshop, and on-topic questions, e.g. familiarity with gender-fair language and MT, to establish relations among participants.

4.2 Stage 1: Problem Storming

A first problem storming session in a cross-community setting of three to four participants per group, where each community was represented, targeted an exchange of experiences, interests, and needs as well as potential challenges in reference to gender-fair (machine) translation. To initiate the discussion, different text samples were provided: descriptions of non-binary people (Example (1)), mixed-gender groups (Example (2)), and without gender indication (Example (3)). For the last two, we provided the English source text with "they" for mixed-gender groups and two MT outputs in German produced with Google Translate and DeepL. The use of colored cards on a pin board was suggested to analyze issues in the (machine) translation of such texts.

(1) Eliot Sumner ist Musiker*in, Schauspieler*in und als Kind von Sting und Trudie Styler quasi im Entertainment-Biz aufgewachsen. Außerdem ist Eliot nichtbinär, identifiziert sich also weder als Mann noch als Frau, weshalb wir hier das nichtbinäre Pronomen "xier" benutzen.

(2) Did someone leave their books here?
   a. Hat jemand seine Bücher hier liegen lassen? (Google Translate & DeepL)

(3) An employee will not do a good job if they don't have the right training.
   a. Ein Mitarbeiter wird keinen guten Job machen, wenn er nicht die richtige Ausbildung hat. (Google Translate)
   b. Ein Mitarbeiter wird keine gute Arbeit leisten, wenn er nicht die richtige Ausbildung hat. (DeepL)

4.3 Stage 2: Utopia Storming

The second stage represented a community-internal group activity and instructs each stakeholder group to jointly dream up a social and technological utopia, where the focus was explicitly not on feasibility but on dreams, hopes, and desires. Here all materials available in the room could be used, including wool, pipe cleaners, etc. At the end of Stage 2, the day concluded with a summary sessions and two Mentimeter word clouds, one on the greatest insights and a second one on the greatest barriers for gender-fair (machine) translation.

4.4 Stage 3: Hands-On

To not go directly from utopias to strategic considerations on the second day, we intercepted the process with a hands-on stage where specific examples of use can be analyzed and the preparatory handout can be put to practice. Cross-community groups of three to four participants obtained profiles of fictional characters, such as Ariel, The Little Mermaid, Peter Pan, Pippi Longstocking (see Fig. 2), with the task to prepare their introduction in gender-fair language. The objective of the activity was to raise awareness on the degree of gender specificity in German, one's own language

Figure 1: Stages for Participatory Workshop on Technology Design

use, and the multiciplity of gender-fair strategies, of which each group was instructed to select one.

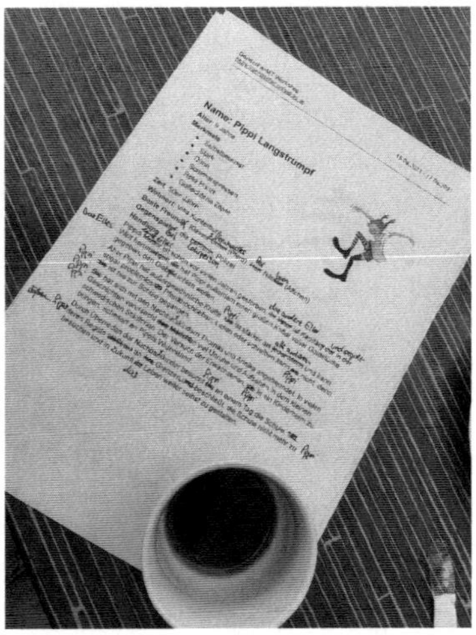

Figure 2: Presenting fictional characters as non-binary

4.5 Stage 4: Strategy Storming

Having identified problems and a desired utopia, the strategy storming stage seeks to gradually turn towards the concrete and potential approaches in an open process endorsing creativity rather than feasibility, which was explicitly described as the focus of the next stage. For this stage, participants were asked to visualize their results, e.g. on flipcharts or with colorful sticky notes.

4.6 Stage 5: Strategizing

Finally, strategizing focuses on the social as well as technical feasibility of discussed strategies. The initial session was a cross-community task within the same grouping as in the strategy storming session. The last day was dedicated to first community-internal sessions on potential cross-fertilization initiatives across communities, followed by a cross-community session on who needs what from whom. At the end of the second day, we asked participants for their preferred gender-fair strategy by means of Mentimeter quizzes.

4.7 Synthesizing

At the end of the third day, a summary of the most central insights and implications was jointly prepared in a plenary session. For a summary at the end of each day as well as for this final summary, we recommend taking notes online live and projecting these notes so that participants can correct potential mistakes directly. Furthermore, the final summary is circulated to participants for inspection, expansion, and correction. To avoid losing the momentum of a successful community building effort and event, concrete steps to interact beyond a sharing of workshop outcomes and further research endeavors should be taken. Following the principles of PAR, a democratic and self-determined method should be foreseen, such as a mailing list, a Wiki, or any other means of interchange of ideas, which at best should be decided together with the participants.

5 Participatory Workshop in Action

A team of ten researchers from Austria conducted a three-day participatory workshop on the topic of gender-fair MT with an initial focus of translating from and to German. Our research team consisted of members of and people closely connected to the queer and non-binary community, professional translators with good contacts in this community, active MT and human-computer interaction researchers with a corresponding network. Thus, we could strongly rely on our personal networks to invite participants and instill the necessary trust for participants to accept the invitation. Participants were additionally recruited through activist groups and open calls, following a sampling strategy that allows for a spread of different marginalized experiences including intersecting aspects of marginalization.

The workshop initially targeted ten participants for each community and stakeholder group. Finally, in total 21 people participated, ten translators, six MT experts, and five queer and non-binary people. Several of these 21 participants had intersectional roles, e.g. translator and MT expert or non-binary and translator. Given that the workshop was organized amidst the pandemic, we were grateful for this turnout and the substantial commitment of participants to take three days off their working week, one MT expert even traveled from Switzerland. To establish a common basis of knowledge, we distributed a preparatory handout summarizing several gender-fair language strategies for German[1]. Additionally, the handout provided pointers for further reading.

In the following we present the results from the workshop activities (see Section 4) by identified problems, proposed utopias, and strategic considerations for realizing gender-fair (machine) translation.

5.1 Problems

In terms of barriers to gender-fair (machine) translation, most participants indicated acceptance, ignorance, lack of resources, and a lack of understanding. One central issue that was identified across stakeholder groups is the linguistic creativity of the German language and the respective higher effort to effect change to achieve gender-fair language use. Ideally, people should be directly asked for their identified pronouns and language strategy, which, however, is practically not feasible for written texts in MT or mixed groups. Participants agreed that numerous linguistic aspects are strongly context-dependent and one general gender-fair language strategy will hardly accommodate all possible contexts. In reference to MT specifically, a lack of gender-fair text samples and training corpora was addressed. Already at this stage first ideas towards solutions were proposed, e.g. to enable users to select the desired gender-fair strategy in the target text and to potentially implement translations from German to gender-fair German as a first step. One central issue unanimously agreed upon is that language alone will not suffice to achieve inclusivity if only linguistic surface forms are changed, but stereotypical gender ideas and reactionary thinking remain unaltered.

5.2 Utopias

Utopia storming in a community-internal setting targeted hopes and dreams of a better, gender-fair world supported by technology, where all available materials could be used. Fig. 3 exemplifies the creativity of the groups, i.e., the MT lego unicorn (a) and the translators' "Eierlegendes Wollmilch Ich-bin-Ich" (egg-laying wool-milk I-Am-Me)[2] (b).

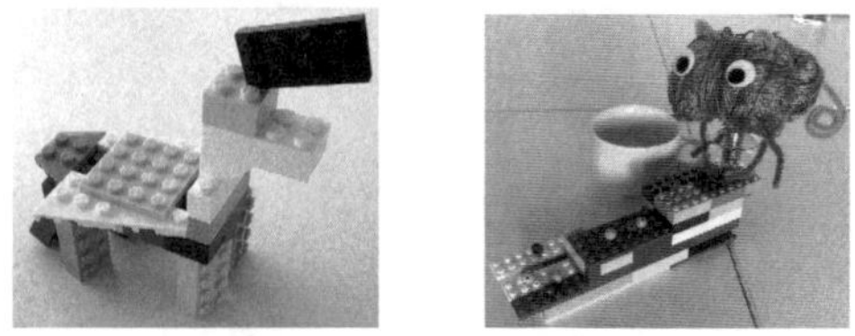

(a) "Leonda, the Gender Avenger" **(b)** "Eierlegendes Wollmilch Ich-bin-Ich"

Figure 3: Shared visualized utopias

The utopia of translators and MT experts advocated guidelines and standards to allow for an easier practical and technical implementation. Standardization could foster acceptance of gender-fair language and simplify language patterns, which could be beneficial to MT. Nevertheless, any standard should be flexible enough to allow for visibility of people disregarded by its necessary reduction. Another interesting idea was a point of contact for gender-fair language, such as a helpline. The utopia of the queer and non-binary group indicated rather a harsh reality, since they desired respect, sensitivity and "just to be able to exist". In the following joint plenary session the necessity of political, legal and social frameworks were discussed as a means to foster the demand for gender-fair language, e.g. to provide incentives for enterprises to achieve specific gender-fair language goals, such as a gender-fair certification mark.

5.3 Strategies

When directly asked about the preferred gender-fair language strategy on the second day, exactly half of voting participants (n=20) preferred gender-inclusive and the other half gender-neutral language. In the hands-on Stage 3, a predominant strategy consisted in omitting pronouns, utilizing names and passive constructions, and substituting nouns with plural or neutral variations, e.g. *Meerjungfrau* (mermaid) became *Meerwesen* (merbeing). Even though for several participants omitting pronouns seemed easier than using neopronouns, e.g. *nin*, this inevitably led to a more frequent repetition of names and subjectively less frequent sentence structures. Two groups utilized the gender-inclusive Dey-E-System[3]. Participants familiar with gender-fair language use found writ-

[1] `https://genderfairmt.univie.ac.at/files/Handout_Genderfaires_Deutsch.pdf`

[2] It reflects on the "eierlegende Wollmilchsau", a colloquialism to indicate something that can cater to all needs exemplified in the unreal animal providing eggs, wool, and milk, and "Das kleine Ich bin ich" (Little I-A-Me) is a reference to a children's book.

[3] As in *einey gute Arzte* (a good doctor); see `https://geschlechtsneutral.net/dey-e-system/`

ing texts from scratch easier than 'translating' an existing profile to gender-fair language, with the argument that gender-specific elements can easily be overlooked. Such involuntary omission is not only a challenge for human beings, but equally for MT, since designing a system that detects infrequent or less obvious mentions, such as *mermaid*, as gender-specific and is capable to provide a gender-fair alternative is definitely an open research issue.

When asked to consciously select a strategy, each group preferred a different solution: (i) a multi-stage model, (ii) the gender-neutral ens strategy, and (iii) the gender-inclusive SYLVAIN system. The idea of a multi-stage model was to clearly assess one's own language use and gradually progress towards gender-fair language. The bottom stage linguistically includes women, e.g. utilizing male and female forms, the German Binnen-I (*LeserInnen*), and only using female forms (*Leserinnen*). The second stage includes non-binary people by utilizing gender-inclusive characters (*, :, _), where MT experts remarked on the issue of * being a syntactic element of technical languages, e.g. to represent text in italics. The final stage aims to avoid outing individuals by linguistic means, which can be achieved with gender-neutral strategies. This idea of a multi-stage model towards gender-fair language could be implemented as a multi-stage MT adaptation process.

The second group preferred the *-ens* strategy as in **Mens**ch (human being), e.g. *Lesens* (reader). Utilizing this strategy would resolve the issue of special characters, character and text length, and pronunciation and readability. Arguments against this strategy were that this form is too similar to the genitive case in German, which might lead to confusions, and that no distinction between singular and plural is foreseen, which leads to further omission of information apart from gender-specific omissions.

The third group preferred the SYLVAIN system that introduces a new gender, the liminal gender, due to a preference of inclusion over omission of gender and with the arguments that contexts can be preserved, direct translation equivalents are facilitated, and a consistent use of language is eased without omissions of information. Nevertheless, translating gender-neutral elements with the SYLVAIN system, e.g. English singular *they* to *nin*, would change the context of the source text and might erroneously assign a liminal gender.

5.4 Strategizing

One suggested solution to overcome the disparity between gender-inclusive and gender-neutral forms was to develop a hybrid form that uses gender-neutral forms and simultaneously permits gender-specific references. However, the criterion of not involuntarily outing individuals might still be an issue in such a hybrid model. In addition to this criterion, practicability, ease of access and pronunciation, universality and acceptability were proposed. To ensure inclusion of diverse groups, including language learners and people with disability, comprehensibility and readability should be taken into consideration. For instance, *Lesx* or *Les** represent gender-neutral language but are neither straightforward to pronounce, comprehend, or apply for first language speakers of German.

From a business perspective, it was deemed essential to achieve and ensure a consistent use of language, e.g. for search engine optimization, whether when writing new contents or translating existing ones. This brought up the idea of standards or guidelines again, which could increase the confidence in grammatical correctness and unify pronunciation. Furthermore, a guideline would ease adoption and support from a social and societal standpoint and equally from an institutional perspective, e.g. major dictionaries of the German language as the Duden, media, or public authorities. Referencing and addressing unknown people would considerably be eased by such standardization, however, such an endeavor is in opposition to the dynamically evolving language and gender-fair language, where strategies are still developing within the queer and non-binary community. As an alternative, flexible guidelines potentially combine a degree of standardization with open possibilities to personalize language.

A reduction of the multiplicity of gender-fair language strategies could ease the generation and availability of gender-fair texts and training data to facilitate MT. In this context, the idea of rule-based generation of text samples and a novel professional profile of a community-based gender-fair pre- and post-editor were discussed. Whether rule-based or implemented differently, MT systems were seen as central tools to explore different approaches to gender-fair language systems.

5.5 Cross-Community Support

In the discussion of mutual support across communities, the translation community suggested jointly creating a cheat sheet for gender-fair language that can be consulted during the translation process, official guidelines to justify translation decisions for clients, training workshops from the queer and non-binary community, and tools to facilitate gender-fair translation. The queer and non-binary community mainly desired gender-fair translations, whether automatically or manually created, to increase gender-fair language use and active and continuous exchange with the other communities, as initiated by this workshop. This community emphasized the role of translators to potentially bridge a gap and facilitate exchange between the majority society and the queer and non-binary community. Furthermore, the community often feels like applicants or solicitors to be included and thus, would desire to be better included and considered by the other communities. The MT community desired mainly gender-fair text samples and corpora and equally a continuous exchange with the other two communities. A continuous involvement of the other communities in the further progress of a gender-fair MT development process was envisioned. In short, communities were united by the desire for interdisciplinary, "multiprofessional" teamwork to jointly work towards the defined objectives. A very nice visual summary that resulted from a final cross-community group session is depicted in Fig. 4.

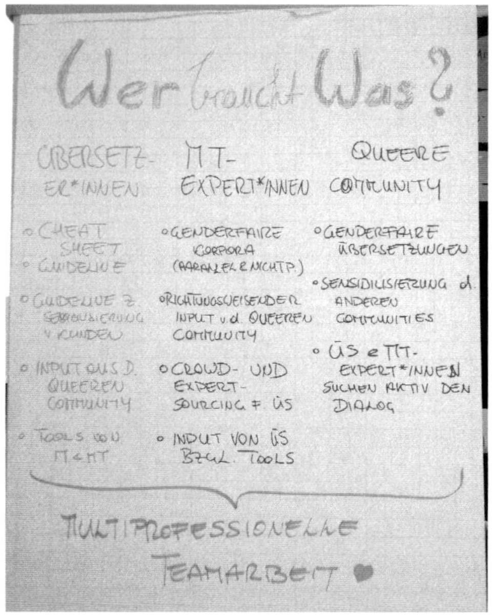

Figure 4: Multi-professional teamwork

6 Reusability of the Participatory Workshop

One option to address a more diversified pool of participants and reach a wider as well as slightly bigger audience could be to move a considerably shortened version of these activities online, as e.g. done by Pannitto et al. (2021) with more tool support for interactive sessions, e.g. Miro to replace flipcharts, breakout groups in video conference tools, etc. Since the nature of PAR projects is to be situated in a particular context and relationships in order to generate situated knowledge, targeting large audiences might benefit from a different methodological choice. Nevertheless, a PAR project provides insights with wider implications from unique use cases, called "communicative generalization" (Cornish, 2020). It addresses the "the significance of knowledge to epistemic communities rather than abstract universal truth" (Cornish, 2020), facilitating the expression and perception of multiple perspectives, enriching the reader's generalized other, and problematizing situations that are taken for granted.

Our case study focused on the issue of gender-fair (machine) translation from English to German as a starting point. While the proposed English materials might be reusable for workshops focused on other languages, adapting the activities to other languages should take culture- and community-specific considerations into account. Nevertheless, we believe that the general method and structure of the workshop can be utilized as a blueprint for further such workshops. On a general note, we recommend alternating group activities, within and across groups of stakeholders, with plenary sessions for joint reflections. Each group should be observed by one team member in a non-participant manner to ensure to take notes on discussions and to intervene should any conflicts or situations of stagnation arise. For plenary sessions, we recommend live summaries that are projected so that participants can directly add/change notes. We provide the core ideas and principles of each activity to facilitate reproducing the workshop in different languages and contexts.

Pre-Workshop Preparation For any given research topic that seeks to involve various, frequently distinct groups of stakeholders, it is vital to ensure that all participants share a common body of knowledge. To this end, a preparatory handout explaining the most essential facts can be distributed to all participants prior to the event. This requires preparing ahead to permit sufficient time for each participant to familiarize themselves with the provided contents. The advantage of this preparatory step is that the workshop can commence with interactive sessions instead of presenting content to participants and participants have the chance to familiarize themselves with the topic at their own pace. Furthermore, it permits time for additional reading in case a single stakeholder feels they would like to know more about a topic – corresponding pointers should be included in the handout.

Warm-Up With sensitive topics, such as gender identity in language, we recommend warm-up activities, such as a sociometric introduction (see Section 4.1), and subtle as well as optional means to identify with a specific group of stakeholders or community.

Stage 1 & 2 At the beginning of the workshop activities, we utilize gender-fair texts and their machine translations to initiate the discussion on potential problems of the topic. These can easily be reproduced for other languages and with any available MT system, since the focus is not on translation adequacy but on triggering a discussion on gender-fair language. Also utopia storming is an easily transferable activity that is best organized offline with a large pool of very different (handicraft) materials, e.g. colorful papers, scissors, building blocks, etc. For this stage, it is important to emphasize that proposed utopias neither need to be possible nor feasible, but could represent any dream vision.

Stage 3 For the hands-on activity, materials need to be adapted to the respective target culture and community. The chosen fictional characters and corresponding profiles should be well known by the participants to be able to present them in gender-fair language, e.g. there might be a better choice than Pippi Longstocking for other settings. For this activity, enough time should be provided for cross-community groups to consider different potential solutions before presenting the one of their choice for the specific fictional character.

Stage 4 After the practical application of strategies, the goal of strategy storming is to consciously think about preferred strategies for (machine) translation and in general. This stage can directly be transferred by adapting the instructions to the specific language.

Stage 5 The final stage seeks to discuss feasible solutions and their socio-technical implications as well as mutually beneficial aspects of community exchange. For this stage, we strongly recommend going from a community-internal to a cross-community group session in order to first discuss ideas within groups of stakeholders and then exchange these among groups. For this stage, materials to visualize thoughts and results are also very important to allow for groups to summarize their main points and sort their ideas.

7 Key MT Implications

As an overview, we summarize the key implications for gender-fair (machine) translation in the following list:

- need for user-centric, customizable selection of gender-fair language strategy in the target language
- gender-fair MT output(s) depend not only on the input but on the context, people addressed, purpose, and user preferences
- potential need to perform intralingual rewriting, e.g. from German to different gender-fair versions of German
- preference to combine gender-neutral with gender-inclusive language to minimize information loss
- awareness that gender-fair language is language-specific and a quickly evolving field, requiring flexible, adaptable solutions
- general criteria to select a gender-fair language strategy, which entail future (psycholinguistic) research:
  - readability and comprehensibility
  - ensuring not to involuntarily out someone
  - practicability and universality
  - ease of access and pronunciation

8 Discussion and Conclusion

As becomes evident from these results, a straightforward decision on a single strategy to ensure linguistic inclusivity is not feasible and this decision should depend on the context – to quote one participant of the workshop "one size fails all". A disparity between a desire to standardize and to personalize gender-fair language brought the discussion to the conclusion that a customizable MT implementation would be most beneficial. It should allow users to flexibly select which strategy to use for a text and, where possible, make informed suggestions for a context-specific strategy.

PAR-based activities gradually brought new arguments from different communities to light and resulted in a catalog of criteria to guide the selection process of gender-fair language strategies for (machine) translation from the multiplicity of dynamically growing proposals, including practicability, ease of access, and universality. Additionally, a central criterion was to provide means of addressing individuals without involuntarily outing their gender identity. Furthermore, any gender-fair language use should be readable, comprehensible, and easy to learn and pronounce. In many cases, gender-neutral strategies, such as *-ens*, comply with these criteria, however, in a translation setting the inherent loss of context-specific information by omitting gender-specific information and plural forms might not be feasible. In a translation setting, a context-preserving target text irrespective of the specific strategy selected was deemed essential as well as further experiments on their translatability.

One central issue with any gender-fair language strategy was a current lack of text samples for training MT systems but also for teaching and exemplifying each strategy, which mostly rely on conjugation and declination tables for their introduction. Hands-on examples clearly showed that any automated method to detect and potentially alter gender-specific mentions in a text needs to go beyond grammatical gender or linguistic surface forms to also detect less obvious examples, such as *mermaid*. To overcome the issue of data for MT, hybrid methods with rule-based elements to synthetically generate text samples were proposed as well as to initiate MT adaptations with a community-informed intralingual system to translate from German to gender-fair German.

In short, this idea of accommodating several gender-fair target texts depending on context and/or user preferences would fundamentally change the current MT paradigm, which relies on the correspondence of one source text with one target text. While the idea of providing different target texts to choose from has entered the world of commercial MT systems, e.g. allowing users to choose between male and female target sentences for a given input, this customization of MT to personalized gender-fair MT target texts would require further substantial adaptations and a community-informed, context-dependent decision on which gender-fair strategies to display if none are indicated by the user. To initiate this development, further research on the selection of gender-fair language strategies that comply with the identified criteria is planned as future work, especially readability and comprehensibility.

As an overall feedback on the workshop, participants were satisfied with the respectful, productive, and constructive atmosphere and there was a general consensus to have gathered new knowledge from the cross-community and community-internal exchanges. Concrete steps for continuing this inter- and transdisciplinary multi-professional teamwork in terms of readability studies and procuring gender-fair text samples have already been initiated. We as organizers were very grateful for the wealth of socio-technical ideas and arguments contributed by participants. We hope that their input will be used to guide future research on gender-fair MT.

References

Attig, Remy. 2022. A call for community-informed translation: Respecting queer self-determination across linguistic lines. *Translation and Interpreting Studies*.

Barker, Meg John and Alex Iantaffi. 2019. *Life isn't Binary*. Jessica Kingsley Publishers, London, UK.

Cadwell, Patrick, Sharon O'Brien, and Carlos S. C. Teixeira. 2018. Resistance and accommodation: factors for the (non-) adoption of machine translation among professional translators. *Perspectives*, 26(3):301–321.

Cornish, Flora. 2020. Communicative generalisation: Dialogical means of advancing knowledge through a case study of an 'unprecedented' disaster. *Culture & Psychology*, 26(1):78–95.

Crawford, Kate. 2017. The trouble with bias. In *Conference on Neural Information ProcessingSystems (NIPS) – Keynote*, Long Beach, USA.

de Sylvain, Cabala and Carsten Balzer. 2008. Die SYLVAIN-Konventionen – Versuch einer "geschlechtergerechten" Grammatik-Transformation der deutschen Sprache. *Liminalis*, 2008(2):40–53.

Fae, Jane. 2016. Non-gendered pronouns are progress for trans and non-trans people alike. *The Guardian*, 14 Dec.

Friedman, Batya and Helen Nissenbaum. 1996. Bias in computer systems. *ACM Trans. Inf. Syst.*, 14(3):330–347, jul.

Friedman, Batya, Peter H. Kahn, Alan Borning, and Alina Huldtgren. 2013. Value sensitive design and information systems. In Doorn, Neelke, Daan Schuurbiers, Ibo van de Poel, and Michael E. Gorman, editors, *Early engagement and new technologies: Opening up the laboratory*, pages 55–95. Springer Netherlands, Dordrecht.

Hayes, Gillian R. 2011. The relationship of action research to human-computer interaction. *ACM Trans. Comput.-Hum. Interact.*, 18(3), August.

Hornscheidt, Lann and Ja'n Sammla. 2021. *Wie schreibe ich divers? Wie spreche ich gendergerecht?: Ein Praxis-Handbuch zu Gender und Sprache*. w_orten & meer, Insel Hiddensee.

Kindon, Sara, Rachel Pain, and Mike Kesby. 2007. *Participatory action research approaches and methods: Connecting people, participation and place*, volume 22. Routledge, New York, NY.

Lardelli, Manuel and Dagmar Gromann. Forthcoming. Translating Non-Binary Coming-Out Reports: Gender-Fair Language Strategies and Use in News Articles. *The Journal of Specialised Translation*.

Martindale, Marianna J. and Marine Carpuat. 2018. Fluency over adequacy: A pilot study in measuring user trust in imperfect MT. *CoRR*, abs/1802.06041.

Pannitto, Ludovica, Lucia Busso, Claudia Roberta Combei, Lucio Messina, Alessio Miaschi, Gabriele Sarti, and Malvina Nissim. 2021. Teaching nlp with bracelets and restaurant menus: An interactive workshop for italian students. *arXiv preprint arXiv:2104.12422*.

Piergentili, Andrea, Dennis Fucci, Beatrice Savoldi, Luisa Bentivogli, and Matteo Negri. 2023. From inclusive language to gender-neutral machine translation. *CoRR*, abs/2301.10075.

Richards, Christina, Walter Pierre Bouman, Leighton Seal, Meg John Barker, Timo O. Nieder, and Guy T'Sjoen. 2016. Non-binary or genderqueer genders. *International Review of Psychiatry*, 28(1):95–102.

Saunders, Danielle and Bill Byrne. 2020. Reducing Gender Bias in Neural Machine Translation as a Domain Adaptation Problem. In *Proceedings of the 58th Annual Meeting of the Association for Computational Linguistics*, ACL 2020, pages 7724–7736, Stroudsburg, PA. ACL.

Savoldi, Beatrice, Marco Gaido, Luisa Bentivogli, Matteo Negri, and Marco Turchi. 2021. Gender bias in machine translation. *Transactions of the Association for Computational Linguistics*, 9:845–874, 08.

Sczesny, Sabine, Magda Formanowicz, and Franziska Moser. 2016. Can gender-fair language reduce gender stereotyping and discrimination? *Frontiers in Psychology*, 7.

Spiel, Katta, Emeline Brulé, Christopher Frauenberger, Gilles Bailley, and Geraldine Fitzpatrick. 2020. In the details: the micro-ethics of negotiations and in-situ judgements in participatory design with marginalised children. *CoDesign*, 16(1):45–65. PMID: 32406393.

Stahlberg, Dagmar, Friederike Braun, Lisa Irmen, and Sabine Sczesny. 2007. Representation of the Sexes in Language. In Fiedler, Klaus, editor, *Social Communication*, Frontiers of Social Psychology, pages 163–187. Psychology Press, New York, NY.

van Anders, Sari M, Zach C Schudson, Emma C Abed, William J Beischel, Emily R Dibble, Olivia D Gunther, Val J Kutchko, and Elisabeth R Silver. 2017. Biological sex, gender, and public policy. *Policy Insights from the Behavioral and Brain Sciences*, 4(2):194–201.

Way, Andy. 2020. Machine translation: where are we at today? In Angelone, Erik, Maureen Ehrensberger-Dow, and Gary Massey, editors, *The Bloomsbury companion to language industry studies*, pages 311–332. Bloomsbury Publishing Plc, London, UK.

Young, Meg, Lassana Magassa, and Batya Friedman. 2019. Toward inclusive tech policy design: a method for underrepresented voices to strengthen tech policy documents. *Ethics and Information Technology*, 21(2):89–103.

Zimman, Lal. 2019. Trans self-identification and the language of neoliberal selfhood: Agency, power, and the limits of monologic discourse. *International Journal of the Sociology of Language*, 2019(256):147–175.

Reducing Gender Bias in NMT with FUDGE

Tianshuai Lu
University of Zurich
tianshuai.lu@uzh.ch

Noëmi Aepli
University of Zurich
naepli@cl.uzh.ch

Annette Rios
University of Zurich
rios@cl.uzh.ch

Abstract

Gender bias appears in many neural machine translation (NMT) models and commercial translation software. Research has become more aware of this problem in recent years and there has been work on mitigating gender bias. However, the challenge of addressing gender bias in NMT persists. This work utilizes a controlled text generation method, Future Discriminators for Generation (FUDGE), to reduce the so-called *Speaking As* gender bias. This bias emerges when translating from English to a language that openly marks the gender of the speaker. We evaluate the model on MuST-SHE, a challenge set to specifically evaluate gender translation. The results demonstrate improvements in the translation accuracy of the feminine terms.

1 Introduction

When we talk about gender bias in neural machine translation (NMT), the first issue that comes to mind is stereotyping, e.g. associating the profession *doctor* with the male pronoun and *nurse* with the female pronoun. While this example does illustrate a clear instance of gender bias, Hardmeier et al. (2021) highlight that it is crucial to recognize that gender bias can manifest in various forms. It becomes essential to determine precisely what is considered harmful, the manner in which it is perceived as harmful, and the specific individuals or groups affected (Savoldi et al., 2021).

Current research on mitigating gender bias in MT often focuses on gender stereotypes

Figure 1: This work focuses on the *Speaking As* bias emerging when translating from English to a language that openly marks the **gender of the speaker** as here in Italian for instance: *sono sicuro/a* ... which translates to "I'm certain ..."

(Stanovsky et al., 2019), translation errors due to speaker gender (Vanmassenhove et al., 2018), or pronoun translation (Loáiciga et al., 2017; Jwalapuram et al., 2020). Furthermore, the proposed methods are often only evaluated on BLEU (Papineni et al., 2002). However, BLEU evaluates on word level and is rather insensitive to specific linguistic phenomena that only affect a few words (Sennrich, 2017).

In this paper, we apply a controlled text generation method, Future Discriminators for Generation (FUDGE) (Yang and Klein, 2021), to mitigate the gender bias that arises when translating from English, a language that marks gender only on pronouns, to Italian, a language that openly marks the gender of the speaker in specific contexts. FUDGE has demonstrated its capabilities on many controlled text generation tasks, e.g. poetry couplet completion, topic-controlled language generation, and machine translation formality change. We further explore FUDGE's performance on a gender-controlled machine translation task.

Furthermore, instead of solely relying on BLEU

Eva Vanmassenhove, Beatrive Savoldi, Luisa Bentivogli, Joke Daems & Janiça Hackenbuchner
Proceedings of the 1st Workshop on Gender-Inclusive Translation Technologes, p. 61–69
Tampere, Finland, June 2023.

(Papineni et al., 2002) as an evaluation metric, we evaluate on MuST-SHE (Savoldi et al., 2022), a novel gender translation challenge set that was built on manually annotated test sets and is specifically designed to measure the translation accuracy of gendered expressions. FUDGE demonstrates improvements in several feminine gender terms' translation accuracy.[1]

2 Bias Statement

In this paper, we explore how to mitigate the mistranslation of feminine gender terms into masculine forms when translating from English to a language that openly marks the gender of the speaker. When an NMT system systematically assumes the gender of the speaker is male, this will cause representational harm, resulting in frequent translation errors for female speakers.

We borrow the systematic classification proposed by Dinan et al. (2020), which classifies gender bias into three dimensions: *Speaking About* (gender of the topic), *Speaking As* (gender of the speaker), and *Speaking To* (gender of the addressee). In this work, we focus on the *Speaking As* bias, which usually appears in first-person sentence translations.

Due to the limitations of annotated data sets, we can only experiment on sentences by male and female speakers. More in-depth research on reducing the representational bias towards non-binary speakers will be possible.

3 Related Work

Controlled Text Generation Some research focuses on fine-tuning a pre-trained model for a desired attribute. Ficler and Goldberg (2017) propose a framework for neural natural language generation (NNLG) controlling different stylistic aspects of the generated text. The method results in a class-conditional language model (CCLM), but it is difficult to separate the desired attribute from the generation model, i.e. the model is usually suitable for one task and needs retraining for another attribute of interest. Keskar et al. (2019) mitigate this issue by proposing a Conditional Transformer Language (CTRL) model that is conditioned on many factors including style, content, and task-specific behavior. However, this is quite expensive. Krause et al. (2021) suggest using discriminators to guide the decoding of LMs. Kumar et al. (2021) propose MUCOCO[2] where they formulate the decoding process as a continuous optimization problem that allows for multiple attributes.

Gender Debiasing A common method to mitigate gender bias is to attach gender tags as proposed by Vanmassenhove et al. (2018). In this case, gender information is integrated into the NMT systems via a tag on the source side. This approach achieves improvements for multiple language pairs. Given the original biased data set, Zhao et al. (2018) propose to construct an additional training corpus where all male entities are swapped for female entities and vice-versa. The goal of the augmentation is to mitigate the bias by training the model on gender-balanced data sets.

Gender Bias Evaluation Bemchmarks Zhao et al. (2018) introduce a benchmark, WinoBias, to measure gender bias in coreference resolution with entities corresponding to people referred to by their occupation. Another benchmark, WinoGender (Rudinger et al., 2018), is a Winograd schema-style (Levesque et al., 2012) set of minimal pair sentences that differ only by pronoun gender. Based on WinoBias and WinoGender, Stanovsky et al. (2019) compose a coreference resolution English corpus that contains sentences in which the subjects are in non-stereotypical gender roles. It is a standard test set to evaluate gender stereotyping in MT. In contrast, MuST-SHE (Savoldi et al., 2022) provides a fine-grained grammatical gender evaluation on word level and gender agreement level, which makes it more suitable to evaluate our model.

4 Method

In a controlled text generation task, it is usually nontrivial to retrain the model $\mathcal{G}$ to condition it on the new attribute a. Yang and Klein (2021) propose Future Discriminators for Generation (FUDGE), a flexible and modular way of conditioning the generative model $\mathcal{G}$ on the desired attribute a that only requires access to the output probabilities of $\mathcal{G}$. FUDGE achieves this by training a binary classifier that predicts at each time step t whether the attribute a will be satisfied in the complete sequence, based on the already generated tokens $y_0 - y_t$.

[1] Code and documentation for the experiments are available on https://github.com/tianshuailu/debias_FUDGE.

[2] The acronym for this algorithm stands for incorporating **mu**ltiple **co**nstraints through **co**ntinuous **o**ptimization.

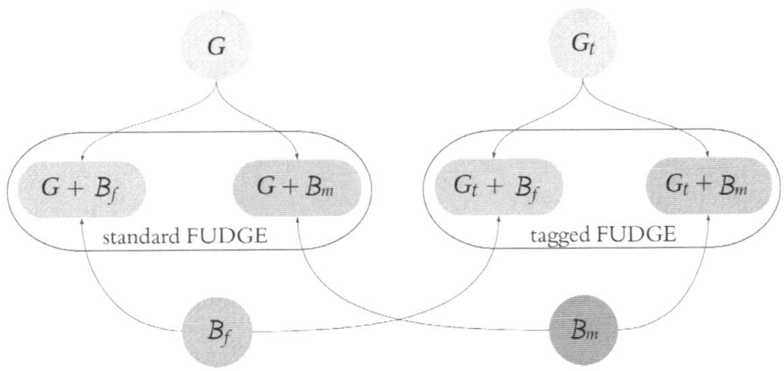

Figure 2: Illustration of four combinations between the underlying translation models $\mathcal{G}$ (translation model trained on original data sets), $\mathcal{G}_t$ (translation model trained on tagged data sets) and two classifiers $\mathcal{B}_f$ (feminine), $\mathcal{B}_m$ (masculine).

To see if gender tags improve FUDGE's performance, we have two underlying English–Italian translation models, $\mathcal{G}$ and $\mathcal{G}_t$. We train both models on the same sentence pairs, with the exception that $\mathcal{G}_t$'s data set includes gender tags on the English source side. The method of adding gender tags is inspired by Vanmassenhove et al. (2018). The desired attributes are feminine and masculine, hence we train two classifiers $\mathcal{B}_f$ and $\mathcal{B}_m$. *Each* of them is combined with the two underlying translation models $\mathcal{G}$ and $\mathcal{G}_t$, resulting in four combinations, as illustrated in Figure 2.

An advantage of FUDGE is the fact that it only needs access to the output logits of the generator model, meaning $\mathcal{G}$ and $\mathcal{G}_t$ can be directly combined with $\mathcal{B}_f$ and $\mathcal{B}_m$ without additional fine-tuning or modification. This allows us to directly use $\mathcal{G}$ and $\mathcal{G}_t$ as baselines.

5 Experimental Setup

5.1 Data

Europarl-Speaker-Information consists of Europarl (Koehn, 2005) tagged with speaker information, including the gender of the speaker. We chose Europarl-Speaker-Information (Vanmassenhove and Hardmeier, 2018) because it contains 44.5% first-person sentences, which makes it suitable for the kind of gender bias the experiments focus to reduce, i.e., *Speaking As*.

ParlaMint 2.1 is a multilingual set of 17 corpora containing parliamentary debates, including gender tags (Erjavec et al., 2021). In Italian, the adjectives and participles are marked with the gender of the speaker in certain grammatical contexts. In the full data set, the utterances where the gender of the speaker is marked are relatively sparse. Hence, we removed sentences that do not contain adjectives or participles for these experiments, since these cannot be marked for the gender of the speaker. The sizes of the original data set and the amount we used are shown in Table 1. In addition, to ensure balanced positive and negative class sizes, we used the same amount of utterances by female and male speakers to train the classifiers.

MuST-SHE v1.2 is a multilingual benchmark allowing for a fine-grained analysis of gender bias in Machine Translation and Speech Translation (Savoldi et al., 2022). MuST-SHE v1.2 contains 656 first-person sentences out of 1073, which makes it suitable for the evaluation of FUDGE.

Table 1 provides an overview of the three data sets along with the information on how they were used in our study. We used the English–Italian part of Europarl-Speaker-Information (Vanmassenhove and Hardmeier, 2018) to train and test the underlying translation models $\mathcal{G}$ and $\mathcal{G}_t$. The monolingual Italian ParlaMint 2.1 corpus (Erjavec et al., 2021) was used to train and test the feminine and masculine classifiers $\mathcal{B}_f$ and $\mathcal{B}_m$. Finally, the English–Italian parallel data from MuST-SHE v1.2 (Savoldi et al., 2022) was used to compare FUDGE and tagged FUDGE against the baselines.

5.2 Training

To get the underlying translation models $\mathcal{G}$ and $\mathcal{G}_t$, we first trim the vocabulary of the pretrained mT5-small (Xue et al., 2021) from HuggingFace (Wolf et al., 2020)[3] to a smaller vocabulary of 25,000

[3]https://huggingface.co/google/mt5-small

		Europarl-Speaker-Information	ParlaMint 2.1	MuST-SHE v1.2
Type		en-it parallel	it monolingual	en-it parallel
#sentences	total	1.29M	996.5k	1095
	used	1.20M	91.6k	1073
M:F ratio	total	2:1	2.5:1	1:1
	used	2:1	1:1	1:1
Usage		train $\mathcal{G}$ and $\mathcal{G}_t$	train $\mathcal{B}_f$ and $\mathcal{B}_m$	evaluation

Table 1: An overview of the language type, gender ratio and the usage of the corpora. Europarl-Speaker-Information (Vanmassenhove and Hardmeier, 2018) English–Italian parallel data sets contain double the amount of utterances by male speakers compared to female speakers and were used to train and test the underlying translation models $\mathcal{G}$ and $\mathcal{G}_t$. ParlaMint 2.1 (Erjavec et al., 2021) Italian monolingual data sets were used to train and test the feminine and masculine classifiers $\mathcal{B}_f$ and $\mathcal{B}_m$. MuST-SHE v1.2 (Savoldi et al., 2022) English–Italian parallel data sets were used to evaluate FUDGE and tagged FUDGE. Both ParlaMint and MuST-SHE data sets that were used for the experiment have an equal amount of utterances by female and male speakers.

	standard FUDGE		*tagged FUDGE*	
	$feminine$	$masculine$	$feminine$	$masculine$
$\lambda = 0$	**27.2**	**27**	**27.5**	**27.1**
$\lambda = 1$	27.1	**27.0**	27.3	26.9
$\lambda = 2$	27.0	26.8	27.2	26.9
$\lambda = 3$	26.9	26.7	27.0	26.7
$\lambda = 4$	26.5	26.6	26.6	26.5
$\lambda = 5$	26.2	26.4	26.2	26.5

Table 2: The BLEU scores of standard FUDGE and tagged FUDGE with both feminine and masculine classifiers, i.e. the four models illustrated in Figure 2. Each model was tested on λ ranging from 1 to 5. When $\lambda = 0$, the classifier does not contribute, hence the first row represents the BLEU scores of the baselines.

English and Italian subword entries.[4] We then fine-tune the trimmed mT5 on the English–Italian part of the Europarl-Speaker-Information (Vanmassenhove and Hardmeier, 2018) data set with adapted example scripts provided in the HuggingFace Transformers repository. $\mathcal{G}$ and $\mathcal{G}_t$ share model architecture and training hyperparameters.

For the two classifiers $\mathcal{B}_f$ and $\mathcal{B}_m$, we use the same amount of filtered sentences by female speakers and male speakers, i.e. 45,800 sentences each.[5] The architecture of the classifier is a 3-layer causal LSTM (Hochreiter and Schmidhuber, 1997) with a hidden dimension of 512. The FUDGE classifiers use the same vocabulary as the generation models (trimmed mT5-small). While it is not mandatory, we choose to initialize the embeddings in the classifier using the pre-trained mT5-small. Alternatively, embeddings can be initialized randomly or using another pre-training method. To train $\mathcal{B}_f$, sentences by female speakers are the positive class, whereas in training $\mathcal{B}_m$, sentences by male speakers are the positive class.

5.3 Evaluation

For evaluation, we use SacreBLEU (Post, 2018)[6] to calculate the BLEU scores. Furthermore, we use

[4]We tokenize 4.5 million English and Italian sentences with the mT5-small tokenizer and keep the 25k most frequent subwords as the trimmed vocabulary.

[5]Filtering based on part of speech (POS): We kept only sentences that contain adjectives and/or participles since those are the only POS that can be marked for the gender of the speaker.

[6]For reproducibility reasons, the version signature is "nrefs:1|case:mixed|eff:no|tok:13a|smooth:exp|version:2.3.1´´

the MuST-SHE challenge set (Savoldi et al., 2022) to assess the models' performance at two levels of granularity, i.e. word-level parts-of-speech (POS) gender evaluation and chain-level gender agreement evaluation. Both POS and agreement chain annotations are on the Italian side.

For word-level evaluation, MuST-SHE performs a fine-grained qualitative analysis of the system's accuracy in producing the target gender-marked words. MuST-SHE computes the accuracy as the proportion of gender-marked words in the references that are correctly translated by the system. An upper bound of one match for each gender-marked word is applied to prevent rewarding over-generated terms.

For agreement-level evaluation, MuST-SHE inspects the agreement chain coverage and translation accuracy. Each agreement chain is composed of several agreement terms. The agreement chain is in coverage only when all the terms appear in the translation (regardless of their gender forms). Then MuST-SHE further evaluates the accuracy of the in-coverage chains. Either the agreement is not respected (*No*), or it is respected with the correct gender (*Correct*) or wrong gender (*Wrong*).

6 Results

6.1 BLEU

Table 2 shows the BLEU scores of standard FUDGE and tagged FUDGE with both feminine and masculine classifiers, i.e. the four models illustrated in Figure 2. The hyperparameter λ determines how much weight is accorded to the classifier's predictions during inference. We test each model with λ ranging from 1 to 5. When $\lambda = 0$, the classifier does not contribute, hence the first row in Table 2 represents the BLEU scores of the baselines. The baselines have the highest BLEU scores for utterances by both female speakers and male speakers. With the increase of λ's value, the BLEU score either does not change or decreases.

6.2 MuST-SHE Gender Translation Evaluation

Word-level Gender Evaluation Table 3 displays the **word-level** feminine and masculine form open-class POS accuracy of standard FUDGE and tagged FUDGE with λ ranging from 1 to 5. The first rows ($\lambda = 0$) display the accuracy scores of the two baselines. *Adj-des* denotes descriptive adjectives. As shown in Table 3a, For both standard and tagged FUDGE, the accuracy of all three feminine form open-class words improves with the increase of λ, while both the baselines and FUDGE maintain high accuracy on masculine form open-class POS, as displayed in Table 3b.

Chain-level Gender Agreement Evaluation Table 4 shows the feminine and masculine **gender agreement** evaluation results of standard FUDGE and tagged FUDGE with λ ranging from 1 to 5, again, the first rows are the accuracy of the baselines. As shown in Table 4a, for the feminine agreement chains, the tagged baseline has more correct agreement chains and less percentage of no agreements than the standard baseline. With the increase of λ, standard FUDGE has more correct agreement chains than tagged FUDGE and a lower percentage of wrong or no agreements. Table 4b illustrates that both the baselines and FUDGE are quite accurate on the masculine agreement chains.

7 Discussion

7.1 BLEU

The first row in Table 2 demonstrates that the tagged baseline improves more on utterances by female speakers, indicating that the advantage of adding a gender tag to the English source side is more noticeable for sentences by female speakers. This result is somewhat expected since there are more utterances by male speakers in the training data, as shown in Table 1, i.e. the model is more likely to produce masculine forms by default.

On the other hand, the BLEU scores of both standard and tagged FUDGE decreases with the increase of λ. Since the classifiers were trained on a relatively small amount of data compared to the generation models, their fluency and grammaticality is not as good. Giving the classifiers more weight during generation while correcting for gender mistakes also makes the output less fluent compared to the mT5-small baselines.

Table 5 illustrates an example of overcorrection: This sentence is uttered by a female speaker, but the translation of the English word, *medium*, *mezzo*, is a noun, not an adjective. However, with high enough λ, FUDGE overcorrects this to a feminine adjective form, *media*.

7.2 MuST-SHE Gender Translation Evaluation

Word-level Gender Evaluation As displayed in Table 3a, for both standard FUDGE and tagged

	standardFUDGE			*taggedFUDGE*		
	Verbs	*Nouns*	*Adj-des*	*Verbs*	*Nouns*	*Adj-des*
baseline	27.4	11.4	35.4	27.3	13.5	36.3
$\lambda = 1$	43.7	12.8	42.9	39.5	13.2	45.7
$\lambda = 2$	60.6	13.2	61.2	56.3	**20.5**	55.1
$\lambda = 3$	62.1	10.8	55.1	63.6	14.3	61.7
$\lambda = 4$	70.1	11.8	61.2	**67.1**	15.4	64.6
$\lambda = 5$	**71.0**	**17.1**	**61.4**	62.9	19.0	**66.0**

(a) The **feminine** form open-class **POS** accuracy

	standardFUDGE			*taggedFUDGE*		
	Verbs	*Nouns*	*Adj-des*	*Verbs*	*Nouns*	*Adj-des*
baseline	87.8	**97.6**	94.3	94.4	**97.6**	94.1
$\lambda = 1$	91.4	96.3	**94.4**	94.5	97.5	92.2
$\lambda = 2$	92.9	97.5	94.2	95.8	97.5	91.7
$\lambda = 3$	94.1	97.4	94.1	93.1	97.5	92.2
$\lambda = 4$	**96.9**	97.5	94.1	**97.0**	97.3	**96.1**
$\lambda = 5$	96.6	97.5	92.0	95.5	97.5	91.8

(b) The **masculine** form open-class **POS** accuracy

Table 3: The feminine and masculine form open-class **POS** accuracy of standard FUDGE and tagged FUDGE with λ ranging from 1 to 5. The first row displays the accuracy scores from the baselines. *Adj-des* denotes descriptive adjectives.

FUDGE, the accuracy of all three open-class words improves, especially for verbs and descriptive adjectives. The classifier helps with the translation of gender-marked terms. As shown in Table 6, the gender of the speaker is female, meaning that the word *sure* needs to be translated into the feminine form *certa* or *sicura*. Both the standard baseline and the tagged baseline translate *sure* to the masculine form *sicuro*, while FUDGE corrects it to *sicura*.

The accuracy of nouns improves with FUDGE, however, the overall accuracy on nouns is much lower than on verbs and descriptive adjectives. A possible explanation is that participles and adjectives refer to the speaker more commonly, and are thus marked with the gender of the speaker, whereas cases where a speaker refers to themselves with a noun (e.g. *I'm a doctor*) are much less frequent in our data sets consisting of parliamentary sessions. Nouns in many cases refer to someone other than the speaker, and thus do not necessarily match the gender of the speaker.

Chain-level Gender Agreement Evaluation The first row of Table 4a shows the agreement chains percentage of the baselines. The tagged baseline performs slightly better than the standard baseline. With the increase of λ, FUDGE improves the percentage of correct agreement chains and reduces the percentage of wrong agreement chains. Furthermore, standard FUDGE performs better than tagged FUDGE.

8 Conclusion

We explore controlled text generation in the context of gender bias by utilizing Future Discriminators for Generations (FUDGE) (Yang and Klein, 2021) in combination with a pre-trained model, mT5-small. Our experiments show that baseline models generally work well on masculine forms since those are much more frequent in the training data Table 1. However, a targeted evaluation reveals that the baselines tend to mistranslate feminine forms. Controlled generation with FUDGE can correct this considerably. Moreover, we observe a trade-off between fluency and gender bias. This is attributed to the fact that our FUDGE classifiers are trained on a relatively small amount of data compared to the generation models. As a con-

	standardFUDGE			*taggedFUDGE*		
	Correct ↑	*Wrong* ↓	*No* ↓	*Correct* ↑	*Wrong* ↓	*No* ↓
baseline	45.5	36.4	18.2	48.6	37.1	**14.3**
$\lambda = 1$	52.8	33.3	13.9	45.7	34.3	20.0
$\lambda = 2$	57.9	28.9	**13.2**	52.6	31.6	15.8
$\lambda = 3$	52.8	27.8	19.4	**56.7**	**27.0**	16.2
$\lambda = 4$	57.1	20.0	22.9	51.3	32.4	16.2
$\lambda = 5$	**63.6**	**18.2**	18.2	44.7	34.2	21.1

(a) **Feminine** gender agreement chain accuracy

	standardFUDGE			*taggedFUDGE*		
	Correct ↑	*Wrong* ↓	*No* ↓	*Correct* ↑	*Wrong* ↓	*No* ↓
baseline	91.1	3.6	5.4	**96.2**	**0.0**	3.8
$\lambda = 1$	94.5	1.8	3.6	94.4	1.9	3.7
$\lambda = 2$	94.4	1.9	3.7	94.2	1.9	3.8
$\lambda = 3$	94.4	1.9	3.7	94.4	1.9	3.7
$\lambda = 4$	**96.5**	**0.0**	**3.5**	**96.2**	**0.0**	3.7
$\lambda = 5$	92.3	**0.0**	7.7	94.7	1.8	**3.5**

(b) **Masculine** gender agreement chain accuracy

Table 4: The feminine and masculine **gender agreement** evaluation results of standard FUDGE and tagged FUDGE with λ ranging from 1 to 5. The first row displays the accuracy scores from the baselines. *Correct* denotes the agreement is respected with the correct gender, *Wrong* denotes the agreement is respected but with the wrong gender, and *No* denotes the agreement is not respected. The numbers represent the percentage of each case.

EN	The internet is a **medium** ...
Ref	Internet è un **mezzo** ...
FUDGE	Internet è un **media** ...
BASE	Internet è un **medio** ...

Table 5: An overcorrection example of tagged FUDGE when $\lambda = 4$ on a sentence by a female speaker. The correct translation of the English word *medium* should be the masculine noun *mezzo*. The baseline uses a wrong masculine noun *medio*, which refers to "middle finger". FUDGE overcorrects *medio* with a feminine noun *media*, means "average value".

sequence, assigning greater weight to their predictions leads to a reduction in fluency and a decrease in BLEU scores. Ideally, the classifiers should be trained on more data. If this is not an option, FUDGE needs to be carefully balanced to obtain improvements without harming the fluency of the translations.

EN	I am **sure** you will agree ...
Ref	Sono **certa** che sarà d'accordo ...
FUDGE	Sono **sicura** che lei concorderà ...
BASE	Sono **sicuro** che lei concorderà ...

Table 6: A correct translation example of tagged FUDGE with $\lambda = 3$ on a sentence by a female speaker. FUDGE translates the English word *sure* into the correct feminine form, *sicura*, while the baseline generates the masculine form, *sicuro*.

Acknowledgements

This work was funded by the EU's Horizon 2020 Programme as part of the project EASIER under grant agreement number 101016982 and the Swiss National Science Foundation project no. 191934).

References

Dinan, Emily, Angela Fan, Ledell Wu, Jason Weston, Douwe Kiela, and Adina Williams. 2020. Multi-dimensional gender bias classification. In *Proceed-*

ings of the 2020 Conference on Empirical Methods in Natural Language Processing (EMNLP), pages 314–331, Online, November. Association for Computational Linguistics.

Erjavec, Tomaž, Maciej Ogrodniczuk, Petya Osenova, Nikola Ljubešić, Kiril Simov, Vladislava Grigorova, Michał Rudolf, Andrej Pančur, Matyáš Kopp, Starkaður Barkarson, Steinhór Steingrímsson, Henk van der Pol, Griet Depoorter, Jesse de Does, Bart Jongejan, Dorte Haltrup Hansen, Costanza Navarretta, María Calzada Pérez, Luciana D. de Macedo, Ruben van Heusden, Maarten Marx, Çağrı Çöltekin, Matthew Coole, Tommaso Agnoloni, Francesca Frontini, Simonetta Montemagni, Valeria Quochi, Giulia Venturi, Manuela Ruisi, Carlo Marchetti, Roberto Battistoni, Miklós Sebők, Orsolya Ring, Roberts Darģis, Andrius Utka, Mindaugas Petkevičius, Monika Briedienė, Tomas Krilavičius, Vaidas Morkevičius, Roberto Bartolini, Andrea Cimino, Sascha Diwersy, Giancarlo Luxardo, and Paul Rayson. 2021. Linguistically annotated multilingual comparable corpora of parliamentary debates ParlaMint.ana 2.1. Slovenian language resource repository CLARIN.SI.

Ficler, Jessica and Yoav Goldberg. 2017. Controlling linguistic style aspects in neural language generation. In *Proceedings of the Workshop on Stylistic Variation*, pages 94–104, Copenhagen, Denmark, September. Association for Computational Linguistics.

Hardmeier, Christian, Marta R. Costa-jussà, Kellie Webster, Will Radford, and Su Lin Blodgett. 2021. How to write a bias statement: Recommendations for submissions to the workshop on gender bias in nlp.

Hochreiter, Sepp and Jürgen Schmidhuber. 1997. Long Short-Term Memory. *Neural Computation*, 9(8):1735–1780, 11.

Jwalapuram, Prathyusha, Shafiq Joty, and Youlin Shen. 2020. Pronoun-targeted fine-tuning for NMT with hybrid losses. In *Proceedings of the 2020 Conference on Empirical Methods in Natural Language Processing (EMNLP)*, pages 2267–2279, Online, November. Association for Computational Linguistics.

Keskar, Nitish Shirish, Bryan McCann, Lav Varshney, Caiming Xiong, and Richard Socher. 2019. CTRL - A Conditional Transformer Language Model for Controllable Generation. *arXiv preprint arXiv:1909.05858*.

Koehn, Philipp. 2005. Europarl: A parallel corpus for statistical machine translation. In *Proceedings of Machine Translation Summit X: Papers*, pages 79–86, Phuket, Thailand, September 13-15.

Krause, Ben, Akhilesh Deepak Gotmare, Bryan McCann, Nitish Shirish Keskar, Shafiq Joty, Richard Socher, and Nazneen Fatema Rajani. 2021. GeDi: Generative discriminator guided sequence generation. In *Findings of the Association for Computational Linguistics: EMNLP 2021*, pages 4929–4952, Punta Cana, Dominican Republic, November. Association for Computational Linguistics.

Kumar, Sachin, Eric Malmi, Aliaksei Severyn, and Yulia Tsvetkov. 2021. Controlled text generation as continuous optimization with multiple constraints. In Beygelzimer, A., Y. Dauphin, P. Liang, and J. Wortman Vaughan, editors, *Advances in Neural Information Processing Systems*.

Levesque, Hector J., Ernest Davis, and Leora Morgenstern. 2012. The winograd schema challenge. In *Proceedings of the Thirteenth International Conference on Principles of Knowledge Representation and Reasoning*, KR'12, page 552–561. AAAI Press.

Loáiciga, Sharid, Sara Stymne, Preslav Nakov, Christian Hardmeier, Jörg Tiedemann, Mauro Cettolo, and Yannick Versley. 2017. Findings of the 2017 DiscoMT shared task on cross-lingual pronoun prediction. In *Proceedings of the Third Workshop on Discourse in Machine Translation*, pages 1–16, Copenhagen, Denmark, September. Association for Computational Linguistics.

Papineni, Kishore, Salim Roukos, Todd Ward, and Wei-Jing Zhu. 2002. Bleu: a method for automatic evaluation of machine translation. In *Proceedings of the 40th Annual Meeting of the Association for Computational Linguistics*, pages 311–318, Philadelphia, Pennsylvania, USA, July. Association for Computational Linguistics.

Post, Matt. 2018. A call for clarity in reporting BLEU scores. In *Proceedings of the Third Conference on Machine Translation: Research Papers*, pages 186–191, Brussels, Belgium, October. Association for Computational Linguistics.

Rudinger, Rachel, Jason Naradowsky, Brian Leonard, and Benjamin Van Durme. 2018. Gender bias in coreference resolution. In *Proceedings of the 2018 Conference of the North American Chapter of the Association for Computational Linguistics: Human Language Technologies, Volume 2 (Short Papers)*, pages 8–14, New Orleans, Louisiana, June. Association for Computational Linguistics.

Savoldi, Beatrice, Marco Gaido, Luisa Bentivogli, Matteo Negri, and Marco Turchi. 2021. Gender bias in machine translation. *Transactions of the Association for Computational Linguistics*, 9:845–874.

Savoldi, Beatrice, Marco Gaido, Luisa Bentivogli, Matteo Negri, and Marco Turchi. 2022. Under the morphosyntactic lens: A multifaceted evaluation of gender bias in speech translation. In *Proceedings of the 60th Annual Meeting of the Association for Computational Linguistics (Volume 1: Long Papers)*, pages 1807–1824, Dublin, Ireland, May. Association for Computational Linguistics.

Sennrich, Rico. 2017. How grammatical is character-level neural machine translation? assessing MT quality with contrastive translation pairs. In *Proceedings of the 15th Conference of the European Chapter of the Association for Computational Linguistics: Volume 2, Short Papers*, pages 376–382, Valencia, Spain, April. Association for Computational Linguistics.

Stanovsky, Gabriel, Noah A. Smith, and Luke Zettlemoyer. 2019. Evaluating gender bias in machine translation. In *Proceedings of the 57th Annual Meeting of the Association for Computational Linguistics*, pages 1679–1684, Florence, Italy, July. Association for Computational Linguistics.

Vanmassenhove, E. and C. Hardmeier. 2018. Europarl datasets with demographic speaker information. In *EAMT 2018 - Proceedings of the 21st Annual Conference of the European Association for Machine Translation*.

Vanmassenhove, Eva, Christian Hardmeier, and Andy Way. 2018. Getting gender right in neural machine translation. In *Proceedings of the 2018 Conference on Empirical Methods in Natural Language Processing*, pages 3003–3008, Brussels, Belgium, October-November. Association for Computational Linguistics.

Wolf, Thomas, Lysandre Debut, Victor Sanh, Julien Chaumond, Clement Delangue, Anthony Moi, Pierric Cistac, Tim Rault, Remi Louf, Morgan Funtowicz, Joe Davison, Sam Shleifer, Patrick von Platen, Clara Ma, Yacine Jernite, Julien Plu, Canwen Xu, Teven Le Scao, Sylvain Gugger, Mariama Drame, Quentin Lhoest, and Alexander Rush. 2020. Transformers: State-of-the-art natural language processing. In *Proceedings of the 2020 Conference on Empirical Methods in Natural Language Processing: System Demonstrations*, pages 38–45, Online, October. Association for Computational Linguistics.

Xue, Linting, Noah Constant, Adam Roberts, Mihir Kale, Rami Al-Rfou, Aditya Siddhant, Aditya Barua, and Colin Raffel. 2021. mT5: A massively multilingual pre-trained text-to-text transformer. In *Proceedings of the 2021 Conference of the North American Chapter of the Association for Computational Linguistics: Human Language Technologies*, pages 483–498, Online, June. Association for Computational Linguistics.

Yang, Kevin and Dan Klein. 2021. FUDGE: Controlled text generation with future discriminators. In *Proceedings of the 2021 Conference of the North American Chapter of the Association for Computational Linguistics: Human Language Technologies*, pages 3511–3535, Online, June. Association for Computational Linguistics.

Zhao, Jieyu, Tianlu Wang, Mark Yatskar, Vicente Ordonez, and Kai-Wei Chang. 2018. Gender bias in coreference resolution: Evaluation and debiasing methods. In *Proceedings of the 2018 Conference of the North American Chapter of the Association for Computational Linguistics: Human Language Technologies, Volume 2 (Short Papers)*, pages 15–20, New Orleans, Louisiana, June. Association for Computational Linguistics.

Gender Neutralization for an Inclusive Machine Translation: from Theoretical Foundations to Open Challenges

Andrea Piergentili[1,2 *], **Dennis Fucci**[1,2 *],
Beatrice Savoldi[1], **Matteo Negri**[1], **Luisa Bentivogli**[1]
[1]Fondazione Bruno Kessler [2]University of Trento
{apiergentili,dfucci,bsavoldi,negri,bentivo}@fbk.eu

Abstract

Gender inclusivity in language technologies has become a prominent research topic. In this study, we explore gender-neutral translation (GNT) as a form of gender inclusivity and a goal to be achieved by machine translation (MT) models, which have been found to perpetuate gender bias and discrimination. Specifically, we focus on translation from English into Italian, a language pair representative of salient gender-related linguistic transfer problems. To define GNT, we review a selection of relevant institutional guidelines for gender-inclusive language, discuss its scenarios of use, and examine the technical challenges of performing GNT in MT, concluding with a discussion of potential solutions to encourage advancements toward greater inclusivity in MT.

1 Introduction

Language technologies have become ubiquitous and play a significant role in our lives. In addition to their benefits, however, these technologies come with potential ethical shortcomings and risks (Blodgett et al., 2020). Among them is gender bias, whose presence in machine translation (MT) is well-documented (Savoldi et al., 2021). Indeed, MT systems were found to systematically prefer masculine forms (e.g., EN *The student* → IT _Lo_ (M) *studente*) and stereotypical gender associations in their outputs (e.g., EN *The doctors and the nurses* → IT _I_ *dottori* (M) *e* _le_ *infermiere* (F)), thus reinforcing bias and reiterating the under-representation of specific groups (Savoldi et al., 2021). As the role of gender is relevant on the social level (Kiesling, 2019) and for each individual's construction of identity (Crenshaw, 1991), the biased behaviors of MT systems give rise to concerns about the consequent risks. These risks rest on the power of language to reproduce and reinforce societal asymmetries (Lazar, 2005), and its impact on our perception (Boroditsky et al., 2003; Gygax et al., 2008).

Spurred by the ever-growing demand for a gender-inclusive language, in this work we explore gender-*neutral* language as a form of gender inclusivity. It conforms to standard and established linguistic resources that allow to avoid gendered forms (e.g., *chairperson* instead of *chairman*) – unlike innovative elements like neopronouns and neomorphemes, which are not considered acceptable in many contexts (see Section 2.1). Comprehensive inquiries on gender-neutral MT are largely absent and its implementation is a substantially uncharted territory. Such gap calls for dedicated work on methodological underpinnings, such as the definition of the objectives and an outline of the main challenges to be faced when developing gender-neutral MT systems.

In light of the foregoing, in the present work we discuss the implementation of inclusive language in MT, through the definition of a novel task for MT: *gender-neutral translation* (GNT). For this purpose, we first provide a brief account of the relation between gender and language, and gender bias in MT (Section 2). Then, we focus on English-Italian translation and start by analysing relevant guidelines for gender inclusivity in both languages to understand the current theoretical

*The authors contributed equally.

frameworks (Section 3). We chose this language pair because it is representative of the challenges faced by MT systems when translating across languages that express gender differently. This mismatch can result in undesired and discriminatory phenomena, such as the misgendering of individuals or stereotyped translations. Thereafter, we integrate the main principles of the guidelines into the context of MT, thus outlining a set of desiderata which define the task of GNT in higher detail (Section 4). Finally, we discuss the open technical challenges that performing and evaluating GNT in MT entails, and examine the potential approaches to address them, thus sketching a road-map towards the implementation of GNT in MT (Section 5).

2 Background

Gender is a complex notion, which has been extensively debated across several disciplines. In the case of language, the relationship with gender is socially relevant (Section 2.1), with an impact on both the visibility of gender groups (Wasserman and Weseley, 2009) and the construction of personal identities (Gygax et al., 2019). Therefore, the appropriate use of gender expressions is critical in communicative practices, including those allowed by language technologies (Section 2.2).

2.1 Gender in Language

The concept of gender is so relevant to human experience that no language lacks expressions of femaleness or maleness altogether (Stahlberg et al., 2007). However, languages differ in how they encode gender. English, for example, is a notional gender language: it expresses the gender of human referents mostly through personal pronouns and possessive adjectives (e.g., *he/him/hers*; *she/her/hers*), and lexically gendered forms (e.g., *man*; *woman*). Grammatical gender languages like Italian, instead, are characterized by a system of morphosyntactic agreement, where several parts of speech beside the noun (e.g., verbs, determiners, adjectives) carry gender inflections, as in *I/Le bambini/bambine sono contenti/contente* (EN *The children are happy*). Such differences are particularly relevant in translation, especially when the source language does not provide gender information about a referent and the target is a grammatical gender language, as in the previous example.

Regardless of cross-lingual differences, however, linguistic practices can be discriminatory when they generate a disparity in the representation of the genders based on normative and stereotypical principles. Androcentric normativity promotes the masculine gender as the human prototype, encompassing the whole human experience (Hellinger and Pauwels, 2007), thus treating women as a gendered deviation from the norm. A typical manifestation of normativity in language is the masculine generic, i.e., the use of masculine forms as conceptually generic, neutral (e.g., *one must watch his language*), when referring to mixed-gender groups or when gender is unknown or unspecified. Stereotypes, instead, are reiterated in the assumption of someone's gender through associations of professional nouns and gender (e.g., *nurse* = feminine, *doctor* = masculine) (He, 2010), fostering unfair gender paradigms. Moreover, within binary gender linguistic frameworks, non-binary experiences are completely omitted from representation.

In light of this, we look at gender-inclusive language[1] for the avoidance of discriminatory language. This is a form of *verbal hygiene* (Cameron, 1995) by which people attempt to regulate language in conformity to certain ideals, and promote linguistic policies that reflect them. The efforts to make language fair and inclusive of all gender identities can be distinguished in two main approaches: *i)* the introduction of innovative linguistic resources , and *ii)* the use of gender-neutral formulations. The first approach is the result of ongoing grassroots efforts, and includes neopronouns (EN *ze/zir* instead of *he/she/him/his/her*), neomorphemes (ES *-e/-es* instead of *-o/-os* and *-a/-as*), and other solutions (e.g., graphemic devices such as IT -@ instead of *-a/-o/-e/-i*) that allow to mention referents without resorting to generic terms. The acceptance of such resources, however, is still highly debated and mostly restricted to informal communication channels like social media (Comandini, 2021). Thus, speakers who wish to use a gender-inclusive language in more formal contexts can turn to the second approach, which solely relies on established gender-neutral devices of the standard language. While some languages already

[1] The label "inclusive language" covers a wide range of linguistic practices aimed at avoiding discrimination and denigration on any basis (see `https://www.apa.org/about/apa/equity-diversity-inclusion/language-guidelines`). Such practices have also been given different labels, such as 'neutral' and 'fair'. To set the object of our analysis within a larger scope of inclusivity, we hereby rely on the label *gender-inclusive language*.

feature convenient gender-neutral resources, such as the well established singular *they* in English,[2] speakers of other languages, such as Italian, cannot rely on similar devices. Then, they can resort to gender-neutralization strategies, such as the preference for epicene words, i.e. words that are not gender-marked and can be used regardless of the referent's gender (e.g., *spokesperson*, as opposed to *spokesman* and *spokeswoman*). Neutralization strategies range from simple word choices to complex sentence formulations without introducing innovative elements, thus being aligned with standardized forms and grammar. Consequently, we look at gender neutralization as a viable and grammatically acceptable form of gender-inclusive language, and a more solid ground for the exploration of gender-inclusive MT.

2.2 Gender (Bias) in Machine Translation

Although affecting many monolingual tasks in natural language processing (NLP), gender bias comes across more evident in cross-lingual scenarios, such as the case of MT, where different languages can encode very different gender marking mechanisms (Prates et al., 2020; Savoldi et al., 2021, *inter alia*). Most efforts to address gender bias in MT still operate in the binary perspective (Vanmassenhove et al., 2018; Stafanovičs et al., 2020, *inter alia*), thus ignoring the neutral solutions. By using gender-neutral forms, it is possible to avoid undue gendering when no information about the referents' gender is available, while also including all gender identities.

Recently, some works have started working on the processing of non-binary gender forms in NLP and highlighted the main challenges involved (Dev et al., 2021; Lauscher et al., 2022). They mainly focused on standard neutral solutions for text classification (Attanasio et al., 2021), coreference resolution (Cao and Daumé III, 2020), and natural language generation tasks, such as gender-neutral rewriting (Sun et al., 2021; Vanmassenhove et al., 2021; Attanasio et al., 2021). As regards MT, Cho et al. (2019) built a benchmark with template sentences to evaluate whether gender neutrality is preserved in Korean → English automatic translations. Working on English → German/Spanish, Saunders & Byrne (2020) also created a benchmark to assess the ability of MT systems to generate neutral target sentences. As the considered target languages do not have a neutral gender, they used gender-neutral placeholders for articles and inflectional morphemes. Finally, specific projects dedicated to gender-inclusive translation are also arising, like GenderFairMT,[3] with a focus on inclusive solutions for English → German MT (Burtscher et al., 2022).

Overall, adopting a neutral translation as a path towards gender inclusivity poses non-negligible challenges to MT. On the one hand, the complexity of implementing neutral forms comes from the inherent difficulties posed by grammatical gender languages, as also exemplified by the case study in (Saunders and Byrne, 2020). On the other hand, the application of an inclusive language must be carefully designed not to be perceived as intrusive nor as language policing.

In light of the foregoing, before we confront the technical challenges that arise from gender-neutralization in MT, we need to lay the groundwork for this endeavor. That is, framing the linguistic possibilities that could be adopted towards an automatic neutral translation, and identifying their suitable deployment.

3 Framing Gender-Inclusive Language

Looking for guidance to determine how MT systems should adopt gender-inclusive language, the MT scenario remains largely unexplored. Nonetheless, several resources intended for (human) communication are available and offer valuable linguistic knowledge for the understanding of gender-inclusive language and towards its adoption in MT. Among the most influential and accessible resources, there are the guidelines produced by renowned institutions to address gender discrimination in language. We consider them 'top-down' approaches in language, as opposed to the 'bottom-up' efforts of grassroots movements. Institutional guidelines currently only address monolingual communication while our domain of interest is translation. However, we analyze them to collect useful inclusive linguistic strategies, which let us investigate GNT and discuss its practical implications. More precisely, we intend to *i)* explore how gender inclusivity is conceptualized within such guidelines (Section 3.1), and *ii)* gain insights concerning *what* should be neutralized and *how* it

[2]See the American Psychological Association's style guidelines: `https://apastyle.apa.org/style-grammar-guidelines/grammar/singular-they`

[3]See `https://genderfair.univie.ac.at/index_en.html`

should be neutralized (Section 3.2).

To this aim, we selected 30 guidelines published online[4] by relevant institutions, equally divided between guidelines for English and Italian (see the full list of guidelines in Appendix A.1). Besides prestige, we prioritized comparability: we selected guidelines by international institutions (e.g., the European Union) that published the same document in both languages, or by national institutions (e.g., universities and governmental bodies) that share a similar status across countries, thus also ensuring that the selected guidelines belong to the same textual genre.

3.1 Conceptualization of Gender

Starting from ***how these inclusive guidelines interpret gender***, and hence gender-based discrimination, we find clear differences between the English and the Italian documents. While the former mostly go beyond the binary gender framework, the Italian guidelines tend to address women and men only. Such a difference emerges clearly in the two versions of the European Parliament's guidelines (see documents E3, I5 in the reference list). This fundamental difference reflects different ideas of discrimination (e.g., E3: "achieving equality", I5: "achieving equality between men and women"). This conceptual discrepancy is reflected in the suggested strategies to address discrimination at the linguistic level. For instance, the Italian guidelines provide extensive lists of feminine counterparts for traditionally masculine professional nouns (e.g., EN *coordinator* as IT *coordinatore* [M] / *coordinatrice* [F]). Also, they often endorse gender specification to avoid masculine generics (e.g., EN *The professors* → *I professori* [M] *e le professoresse* [F]). Since such suggestions remain within a binary framework, they do not conform to our gender-neutral goal, and are hence discarded in the following discussion.

3.2 Neutralization Strategies

Moving on to the gender-neutralization strategies, here we discuss them through a multilingual perspective, focusing on their practical implications. In Table 1, we also offer a systematization that attempts to map strategies across English and Italian – except for highly language-specific solutions that are impossible to transfer.

[4]Retrieved through Google queries on October 28, 2022.

Concerning ***what should be neutralized***, we identify that these documents tend to largely focus on a particular form of gender discrimination: masculine generics. Masculine generics have been historically employed in administrative/legal texts to briefly refer to the public at large (e.g., see example B, where *he* refers to the whole occupational category of *judges*, and the Italian *il docente* [M], *professor* for the full teaching body). In the same vein, stereotypical associations and androcentric forms are discouraged (e.g., see example A in English). Overall, these guidelines are mostly concerned with generic referents. As we will discuss in Section 4, however, there are also circumstances where avoiding gender marks is necessary, e.g., to avoid misgendering individuals. Finally, and from a linguistic standpoint, we underscore that – as expected – English gender-inclusive strategies focus on the neutralization of pronouns (e.g., C, E), which are the main carrier of gender distinction in notional languages. Instead, the Italian guidelines prioritize the neutralization of nouns thus overlooking adjectives, pronouns, and verbs, which are subject to gender agreement too. Although the analyzed sentences are simple toy examples within an institutional genre, effective gender-inclusive solution should take into consideration the full range of gendered words in grammatical gender languages.

In light of the foregoing, we now delve into ***how to avoid gender discrimination in language***. As previously anticipated, these top-down guidelines advocate for the use of neutralization strategies that conform to standardized, institutional language, over innovative, uncertain forms. As shown in Table 1, neutral solutions can vary greatly, ranging from omissions (e.g., E), and simple replacements of single words with epicene or collective nouns (e.g., A, B, D), to more complex reformulations that involve structural changes at the sentence level (e.g., F, G, H, I). On the one hand, though elegant, nouns replacement might be limiting if other gender-marked words are present, and only allow for a partial neutralization, e.g., as in IT ***Il*** [M] ***professore*** [M] ***è tenuto*** [M] *a rispondere* (EN *The professor must answer*) neutralized as ***L'insegnante è tenuto*** [M]. Moreover, the contextual nature of synonymy makes the choice of gender-neutral alternatives strictly case-specific (Edmonds and Hirst, 2002). When possible, however, the neutralization of short segments appears

A. Epicene synonyms		
EN	E5	*Chairman* → Chair(person)
IT	I3	*Professore* [Professor] → Docente [Teacher]
B. Pluralization (towards generic or epicene forms)		
EN	E2	A judge must certify that *he* has familiarized *himself* with... → All judges must certify that they have familiarized themselves with...
C. Relative and indefinite pronouns		
EN	E5	If a staff member is not satisfied..., *he* can ask for a rehearing. → Any staff member who is not satisfied... can ask for a rehearing
IT	I3	L'assicurazione... è a carico *del fruitore* [of the user]. → a carico di chi fruisce [of who uses].
D. Collective and Role nouns		
EN	§	Please contact one of the *waiters*. → Please contact our staff.
IT	I3	Il palazzo ospita gli studi *dei professori* [of the professors] di slavo. → Il palazzo ospita gli studi del personale docente [of the teaching staff] di slavo.
E. Omission		
EN	§	A person must reside... before *he* may apply for permanent residence. → ...before _ applying for permanent residence.
IT	I3	Un'accurata compilazione facilita *allo studente* [to the student] diverse → ...facilita _ diverse operazioni.
F. Repetition		
EN	E3	A manager may apply... if permission has been granted by *his* institution. → ...if permission has been granted by that manager's institution.
G. Passive voice		
EN	E5	Each action officer must send *his* document. → Documents must be sent.
IT	I1	*Il* richiedente presenta la domanda [The applicant submits the application]. → La domanda va presentata [The application must be submitted].
H. Imperative forms		
EN	E5	Each staff member is requested to submit *his* information. → Please submit all information.
IT	§	*Il cittadino* deve allegare [The citizen must attach] un documento. → Allega [Attach] un documento.
I. Impersonal forms		
IT	I15	*Il candidato* decade [The candidate loses] dal diritto... → Si decade [*One loses] dal diritto...

Table 1: Examples of neutralization strategies. In *red, italic* the generic masculine formulations; in green, underlined the gender-neutralizations. Column 2 provides the reference to the (E)nglish/(I)talian guidelines where each example was found (E1,2,3,..). If no example was found for a specific strategy within the guidelines, but the strategy is nonetheless be applicable, we fabricated an example (indicated with §). If a strategy is not applicable in one language, the corresponding example was omitted.

preferable as it makes the outcome more fluent, as opposed to more complex phrasings. This strategy is not always viable, though. Consider, for instance, the Italian term "*figlio/a*" (EN *child*): in lack of epicene synonyms, neutralization would require verbose periphrases, e.g., IT *minore a carico* (EN *underage, dependent child*) or *persona che si è concepita o adottata* (EN *person who was conceived or adopted*).

Neutralization strategies emerge as complex choices, to be carefully selected and weighted so as to preserve the effectiveness of communication and the acceptability of a text, i.e, features like fluency, style. Such choices, of course, highly depend on various constraints (e.g., register, length, context of use). Therefore, when adopting inclusive language, it is crucial to consider the possible trade-off between neutrality and the overall acceptability of the text where it is implemented. Moreover, as previously discussed, the feasibility and efficacy of adopting neutral strategies heavily depends on the context and the content of the source text. Therefore, such strategies are expected to be particularly pertinent in certain contexts, such as the administrative-institutional domain – to which, it is worth noting, most monolingual guidelines belong. Different and less formal textual styles and contexts could present harder challenges in performing GNT because of the higher heterogeneity of their texts, where the strategies presented above might prove inapplicable or inappropriate. For instance, consider the translation of the simple, colloquial sentence EN *I have never been there* into Italian (*Non sono mai stato/stata lì*): none of the strategies in Table 1 is applicable here. However, compared to institutional and administrative communication, colloquial contexts tend to have greater tolerance to creative translations (e.g., IT *Non ho mai messo piede lì* – literally, EN *I have never set foot there*). Whether the system should resort to similar (or other) devices when straightforward solutions such as the strategies discussed above are not applicable is a decision that should be taken into account when building inclusive MT systems.

4 Desiderata for GNT in MT

In light of both the insights that emerged in Section 3, we now specifically address the use case of GNT, which allows MT systems to avoid discriminatory practices while conforming to standard linguistic forms. Specifically, **we define GNT as the task of automatically translating from one language into another without marking the gender of human referents in the target.** For example, given the English sentence *Your neighbors will thank you*, an inclusive MT system is required to translate *Il vostro vicinato*[5] *vi ringrazierà*, as opposed to *I vostri vicini vi ringrazieranno*, which features a masculine generic.

One crucial aspect of GNT is to determine when it should be performed, namely, when the marking of gender should be avoided or preferred. To this aim, and informed by our analysis of the existing guidelines, we devise three main desiderata to obtain a gender-neutral MT output, with specific examples in Table 2.

D1. Gender should not be expressed in the output translation when it cannot be properly assumed in the source. An inclusive MT system is expected to perform a gender-neutral translation in the target language when the gender of the referent(s) cannot be properly assigned from the source. This scenario is quite frequent when translating from a notional gender language into a grammatical gender one, because of the gap in gender expression we discussed in Section 2.1. In these cases a gender-neutral translation refrains from any gratuitous assumptions, thus avoiding expressions which may: *i)* misgender a specific referent (Example 1); *ii)* exclude a social group, such as in the case of masculine generics (Ex. 2); *iii)* foster stereotypical associations (Ex. 3); adopt "androcentric" expressions (Ex. 4).

D2. Proper expressions of gender should be generated in the output translation if they are (indirectly) expressed in the source. The gender of some entities can be sometimes inferred through linguistic elements, which we may define as "gender cues". For example, in English, gender cues are 3rd person pronouns (*he/him/his*, *she/her/hers*), terms of address (e.g., *Mr./Mrs/Ms.*), gender-specific nouns (e.g, *boy, lady, lord, wife*). The presence of gender cues is crucial in determining whether a GNT is required or not. In (Ex. 5), the pronoun *herself* unequivocally identifies the referent as feminine. First names, surnames, or even nicknames, however, should not be included among these cues for several reasons. First names can hardly be considered a reliable index of someone's gender identity (Lauscher et al., 2022). Even in the attempt of any binary correlation, names and nicknames are highly ambiguous across genders and cultures (e.g., *Andrea*, which is typically masculine in Italian, but feminine in German). In addition, referents' gender could be known also through non-textual elements, such as explicit external information about who is speaking, which is sometimes provided to the translators. In all these cases, gender expressions are preferable in the translation.

D3. Masculine generics should not be propagated from the source language to the output translation. In spite of the seemingly straightforward definition of gender cues in D2, their recognition might not be clear-cut. This is the case of masculine generics used in the source, whose distinction from an actual gender cue might be equivocal. Hence, a MT system should be brought to carefully consider every information, in particular the word *man* along with its derivations and compounds so as to understand if they are used properly. For instance, to explicitly refer to the

[5]While the word *vicinato* is formally masculine, as a collective noun it is conceived as conceptually neutral.

(1)	EN	I refuse to give up on **a single student** in my class.
	IT	Mi rifiuto di lasciare indietro *un solo* studente nella mia classe.
	GNT	Mi rifiuto di lasciare indietro qualsiasi studente nella mia classe.
(2)	EN	**A lot of innovative teachers** began bringing comics...
	IT	*Molti* insegnanti *innovativi* iniziarono a portare i fumetti...
	GNT	Un gran numero di insegnanti all'avanguardia iniziarono a portare i fumetti...
(3)	EN	We train **nurses** to do it, and they use local anesthetics.
	IT	Formiamo *le infermiere* a farlo, e loro usano anestetici locali.
	GNT	Formiamo il personale infermieristico a farlo, e loro usano anestetici locali.
(4)	EN	Vehicles may only proceed **at walking pace**.
	IT	I veicoli possono procedere solo *a passo d'uomo*.
	GNT	I veicoli possono procedere solo a passo di persona.
(5)	EN	Even **the lead singer herself** abandoned the project.
	IT	Persino la stessa cantante solista ha abbandonato il progetto.
(6)	EN	It affects one to two percent of the population, more commonly **men**.
	IT	Riguarda dall'uno al due percento della popolazione, ed è più comune negli uomini.
(7)	EN	Earth was pristine before **men** appeared.
	IT	La Terra era incontaminata prima della comparsa *degli uomini*.
	GNT	La Terra era incontaminata prima della comparsa degli esseri umani.
(8)	EN	The **fishermen** were so upset about not having enough fish to catch that...
	IT	I *pescatori* erano così *disperati* per la mancanza di pesce da pescare che...
	GNT	Le persone che pescavano erano così disperate per la mancanza di pesce da pescare che...
(9)	EN	Now when I was a **freshman** in college, I took my first biology class.
	IT	Quando ero uno studente al primo anno di università, seguii il mio primo corso di biologia.

Table 2: Examples for D1-3. We mark binary gender-marked expressions in *red*, and in green those that are neutral.

masculine gender group as a whole (Ex. 6), where a neutralization would effectively compromise the meaning of the sentence. On the contrary, when they are used to refer to the totality of human beings (Ex. 7), or to entire categories of mixed-gender people through terms such as *fishermen* (Ex. 8), thus effectively functioning as masculine generics, they should be translated with neutral forms in the output. As there is not always a clear-cut distinction between a masculine generic and a masculine term used to refer to an actual masculine referent, and given the short context window within which MT systems operate, ambiguous cases can occur rather frequently. In these cases, a GNT should be considered the safest option as it avoids the propagation of the potential masculine generic without compromising the meaning of the sentence. Nonetheless, there is a specific case where gender cues ought to be considered as trustworthy; namely, in relation to the speaker as 1st person singular referent (Ex. 9). Based on the assumption that speakers deliberately choose the most appropriate expressions while talking about themselves, such a choice should be respected in the output translation.

In conclusion, we have outlined a set of three overarching desiderata towards the purpose of gender-inclusive MT. Such a scaffolding represents our proposed set of guiding principles to be applied towards the development of more inclusive MT models based on gender-neutral translation. In the next Section, we discuss the technical challenges of implementing such desiderata in MT.

5 Challenges and Insights for a Gender-Neutral Machine Translation

The adoption of neutral forms in MT could be conceived as a condition to be met or not met, without any intermediate nuance. The efficacy with which the condition is satisfied, on the contrary, can be rather nuanced; for example, there might be alternative inclusive solutions which might be perceived as more elegant or semantically closer to the input text, and others that satisfy these conditions to a lesser extent. Therefore, from a formal perspective, gender inclusivity can be likened to the concept of *constraint* (Garbacea and Mei, 2022).

As a constraint, it shows a multifaceted character, which makes it comparable to other types of well-known constraints adopted in automatic language generation (Garbacea and Mei, 2022). First, as seen in Section 3, gender inclusivity can be linguistically realized through both specific lexical forms and syntactic constructions. For this reason, it can be likened to *lexical* and *syntactic constraints*. Then, the requirement of producing automatic translations that are as readable and fluent as possible, which is not always easily guaranteed in the case of neutral reformulations, makes gender inclusivity analogous to *utility constraints* (i.e. the criteria by which a text must exhibit characteristics such as coherence, comprehensibility, and faithfulness) (van Deemter, 2009). Nevertheless, gender inclusivity also summarizes the manifold challenges of the aforementioned constraints, thereby demonstrating a higher level of complexity. Below we illustrate the major challenges of satisfying such a multifaceted constraint, focusing on the dynamicity of the neutralization strategies (Section 5.1), the dearth of adequate training data and methods (Section 5.2), and the lack of evaluation procedures (Section 5.3).

5.1 Addressing the Dynamic Nature of Gender Inclusivity

To prevent unintended neutralizations, it is not always advisable to ensure GNT at all times (see Section 4). This condition makes neutral translation a "dynamic constraint", requiring MT systems to determine when to apply GNT. This ability, however, may be challenging to acquire, especially when gender cues are available outside the limited sentence context (e.g., *He was talking with a young man. Only later I realized that this person was a professor*). This presents a problem for current state-of-the-art MT systems, which work at the sentence level, i.e., by translating each sentence in isolation.

Alternative solutions that account for larger textual context in translation (Lopes et al., 2020) might be more apt to decide when performing neutral translations. For example, the design of MT models that translate beyond the sentence level ought to be considered. Translating sentences in a wider context, indeed, has proven crucial for correctly handling discourse cohesion (Bawden et al., 2018), and was shown to a certain extent beneficial to mitigate gender bias (Basta et al., 2020). However, it remains occasionally dubious whether context provides a useful linguistically-motivated knowledge (Kim et al., 2019; Li et al., 2020). Before venturing into any document-level endeavor, it is thus recommended to verify whether there is a positive interpretable link between gender-neutral translation, context-informed MT, and overall quality of the system.

Besides gender cues, explicit external information too may contribute to the disambiguation of gender in the source sentence, thus guiding the neutral translation. For instance, speakers' metadata can be supplied in the form of tags, either at the word level (Stafanovičs et al., 2020) or at the sentence level (Vanmassenhove et al., 2018; Basta et al., 2020). Such prior knowledge, therefore, can also provide assistance in addressing the dynamic nature of gender inclusivity.

5.2 Constraining MT systems towards GNT

Future GNT-capable models are expected to learn to map words referring to human referents to corresponding neutral translations in order to satisfy the desiderata D1-3. Ideally, these models should be able to learn this mapping based on extensive training sets that include pairs of sentences with gender-neutral translations. To the best of our knowledge, however, training data that consistently have neutral forms in the target side (with a grammatical gender language as target) is lacking. It is necessary, then, to think of training methods that can overcome this lack of data, for example by taking inspiration from methods already applied to MT to satisfy other types of constraints.

Although various strategies have been proposed to make systems meet constraints (for an overview see (Garbacea and Mei, 2022)), it is crucial to evaluate which ones are applicable to the objective of gender inclusivity and how they can be adapted accordingly. The most straightforward method, for example, is to make the constraint explicit to the model directly in the input data. In the case of lexical constraints, this has been done by appending the constraint in the form of a target word or lemma to the source input so as to encourage the model to copy it in the output (Dinu et al., 2019; Song et al., 2019; Chen et al., 2020, *inter alia*). However, this approach is designed to work mainly at word-level, hence it would not be suitable when neutralization should involve several segments of the sentence. Moreover, this method requires bilingual dictionaries to map source words to target words. For gender inclusivity, however, such terminologies are not available, yet. Upon their creation, this technique could be taken into account when dealing with neutral source words which may be suitably translated with target epicene words.

Another line of solutions consists in restricting the search space at decoding time to sequences that contain the pre-defined constraints, such as specific words or phrases in the lexically-constrained MT. For example, Hokamp & Liu (2017) and Post & Vilar (2018) proposed modified versions of the beam search, which ensure that the translation hypotheses have met all the constraints before concluding the search. Similarly, Saunders & Byrne (2020) and Saunders et al. (2022) designed a constrained beam search pass to improve gender diversity – but for masculine/feminine forms only – in the n-best list by producing synthetic gendered alternatives of the original best hypothesis. Alternatively, some approaches were proposed to re-rank the n-best hypotheses according to additional scores, which informed whether or to which extent the constraints were satisfied, like in the dubbing-optimized MT (Saboo and Baumann, 2019) or in gender-specific translations (Saunders et al., 2022). Decoding and re-ranking methods, however, may also entail outputs of lower quality (Saboo and Baumann, 2019; Chousa and Morishita, 2021), due to the restriction of the search space and the trade-off between the need to satisfy the constraint and to faithfully reproduce the source text. Therefore, although such approaches may be a promising way to ensure gender inclusivity in automatic translations, their adoption too should be carefully evaluated.

5.3 Evaluating Gender-Neutral Outputs

The lack of dedicated test sets and metrics prevents the possibility of determining whether systems are actually making any advancements towards the resolution of a given task. In the case of gender-neutral MT, the benchmarks – traditionally designed as parallel data for reference-based evaluations – should comprise a range of source sentences aligned with target ones expressing either gender-marked or gender-neutral forms. As a suitable starting point, the domain of such a test set could be based on the institutional/administrative texts, since the guidelines available for gender-inclusive language belong to this domain (see Section 3). In addition to parallel data, specific protocols should also be designed to effectively evaluate whether the neutrality constraint has been satisfied.

Typically, MT evaluation methods involve comparing the output with a reference and measuring the degree of overlap between n-grams (Papineni et al., 2002; Popović, 2015) or the distance between the generated sentence and the reference in terms of edit operations required to make them equal (Snover et al., 2006). Some more sophisticated metrics take into account not only exact matches but also stems, synonyms, and paraphrases when comparing the MT output with the reference translation (Banerjee and Lavie, 2005). Alternatively, neural metrics use models to predict the similarity between the output and reference (or even directly between the source and output) (Rei et al., 2020). Although metrics that do not rely solely on surface similarity may be more appropriate for evaluating gender neutrality, it may be preferable to develop accuracy-like scores that isolate the evaluation of gender neutrality from the overall translation quality. This could involve annotating such expressions in the reference translation and attempting to match them, as done in MuST-SHE (Bentivogli et al., 2020). In such cases, accuracy is determined through string matching between expressions in the reference and in the output. Hence, the risk of mismatch remains present, as automatic neutralizations may be difficult to detect in an evaluation pipeline based on a single reference and may require extensive manual analysis to be identified (Savoldi et al., 2022). Using multiple references (Qin and Specia, 2015) that contain different neutral realizations to account for language variability could alleviate this difficulty. Another option would be to calculate accuracy without exploiting reference translations, as designed in WinoMT (Stanovsky et al., 2019). In WinoMT the aim is to identify the gendered translation through word alignment with the source, determine its gender through a morphological analyzer, and then check whether it corresponds to that of the source. However, our scenario includes an additional challenge, as in grammatical gender languages gender-neutral expressions may carry a formal gender (e.g. *la persona interessata* is a gender-neutral alternative of the masculine generic *interessato*, but it is formally feminine). Thus morphological analysis may be problematic.

Overall, effectively evaluating whether the output of an MT system is gender-neutral or gender-marked presents several challenges. These challenges need to be addressed to develop an accurate approach that can overcome the limitations of overall translation quality metrics and account for the intrinsic variability of gender-neutral solutions.

6 Conclusions

As a promising route forward to counter gender bias, in this work we have taken the first steps towards the adoption of gender-inclusive language in MT, focusing on the use of neutral forms devoid of gender marking for an English-Italian setting. To this aim, we reviewed various gender neutralization strategies presented in English and Italian guidelines for inclusivity, and outlined a definition of gender-neutral translation (GNT). Finally, we identified and discussed the technical challenges involved in implementing GNT in MT.

7 Acknowledgements

This work is part of the project "Bias Mitigation and Gender Neutralization Techniques for Automatic Translation", which is financially supported by an Amazon Research Award AWS AI grant.

Moreover, we acknowledge the support of the PNRR project FAIR - Future AI Research (PE00000013), under the NRRP MUR program funded by the NextGenerationEU.

References

Attanasio, Giuseppe, Salvatore Greco, et al. 2021. E-mimic: Empowering multilingual inclusive communication. In *IEEE Big Data 2021*, pages 4227–4234.

Banerjee, Satanjeev and Alon Lavie. 2005. METEOR: An automatic metric for MT evaluation with improved correlation with human judgments. In *ACL Workshop on Intrinsic and Extrinsic Evaluation Measures for Machine Translation and/or Summarization*, pages 65–72.

Basta, Christine, Marta R. Costa-jussà, and José A. R. Fonollosa. 2020. Towards mitigating gender bias in a decoder-based neural machine translation model by adding contextual information. In *The Fourth Widening Natural Language Processing Workshop*, pages 99–102.

Bawden, Rachel, Rico Sennrich, et al. 2018. Evaluating discourse phenomena in neural machine translation. In *16th NAACL HLT*, pages 1304–1313.

Bentivogli, Luisa, Beatrice Savoldi, et al. 2020. Gender in Danger? Evaluating Speech Translation Technology on the MuST-SHE Corpus. In *58th ACL*, pages 6923–6933.

Blodgett, Su Lin, Solon Barocas, et al. 2020. Language (Technology) is Power: A Critical Survey of "Bias" in NLP. In *58th ACL*, pages 5454–5476.

Boroditsky, Lera, Lauren A. Schmidt, and Webb Phillips. 2003. Sex, syntax, and semantics. In Getner, Dedre and Susan Goldin-Meadow, editors, *Language in Mind: Advances in the Study of Language and Thought*, pages 61–79. MIT Press.

Burtscher, Sabrina, Katta Spiel, et al. 2022. "Es Geht Um Respekt, Nicht Um Technologie": Erkenntnisse Aus Einem Interessensgruppen-üBergreifenden Workshop Zu Genderfairer Sprache Und Sprachtechnologie. In *Mensch Und Computer 2022*, page 106–118.

Cameron, Deborah. 1995. *Verbal Hygiene (The Politics of Language*. Routledge.

Cao, Yang Trista and Hal Daumé III. 2020. Toward gender-inclusive coreference resolution. In *58th ACL*, pages 4568–4595.

Chen, Guanhua, Yun Chen, et al. 2020. Lexical-constraint-aware neural machine translation via data augmentation. In *29th IJCAI*, pages 3587–3593.

Cho, Won Ik, Ji Won Kim, et al. 2019. On Measuring Gender Bias in Translation of Gender-neutral Pronouns. In *First Workshop on Gender Bias in Natural Language Processing*, pages 173–181.

Chousa, Katsuki and Makoto Morishita. 2021. Input augmentation improves constrained beam search for neural machine translation: NTT at WAT 2021. In *8th Workshop on Asian Translation*, pages 53–61.

Comandini, Gloria. 2021. Salve a tuttə, tutt*, tuttu, tuttx e tutt@: l'uso delle strategie di neutralizzazione di genere nella comunità queer online. : Indagine su un corpus di italiano scritto informale sul web. *Testo e Senso*, 23:43–64.

Crenshaw, Kimberle Williams. 1991. Mapping the margins: Intersectionality, identity politics, and violence against women of color. *Stanford Law Review*, 43(6):1241–99.

Dev, Sunipa, Masoud Monajatipoor, et al. 2021. Harms of Gender Exclusivity and Challenges in Non-Binary Representation in Language Technologies. In *EMNLP 2021*, pages 1968–1994.

Dinu, Georgiana, Prashant Mathur, et al. 2019. Training neural machine translation to apply terminology constraints. In *57th ACL*, pages 3063–3068.

Edmonds, Philip and Graeme Hirst. 2002. Near-synonymy and lexical choice. *Computational Linguistics*, 28(2):105–144.

Garbacea, Cristina and Qiaozhu Mei. 2022. Why is constrained neural language generation particularly challenging? *ArXiv e-prints arXiv:2206.05395*.

Gygax, Pascal M., Ute Gabriel, et al. 2008. Generically Intended, but Specifically Interpreted: When Beauticians, Musicians and Mechanics are all Men. *Language and Cognitive Processes*, 23:464–485.

Gygax, Pascal Mark, Daniel Elmiger, et al. 2019. A Language Index of Grammatical Gender Dimensions to Study the Impact of Grammatical Gender on the Way We Perceive Women and Men. *Frontiers in Psychology*, 10.

He, Guimei. 2010. An analysis of sexism in english. *Journal of Language Teaching and Research*, 1(3):332–335.

Hellinger, Marlis and Anne Pauwels, editors. 2007. *Handbook of Language and Communication: Diversity and Change*. De Gruyter Mouton.

Hokamp, Chris and Qun Liu. 2017. Lexically constrained decoding for sequence generation using grid beam search. In *55th ACL*, pages 1535–1546.

Kiesling, Scott F. 2019. *Language, Gender, and Sexuality: An introduction*. Routledge.

Kim, Yunsu, Duc Thanh Tran, and Hermann Ney. 2019. When and Why is Document-level Context Useful in Neural Machine Translation? In *Fourth Workshop on Discourse in Machine Translation*, pages 24–34.

Lauscher, Anne, Archie Crowley, and Dirk Hovy. 2022. Welcome to the Modern World of Pronouns: Identity-Inclusive Natural Language Processing beyond Gender. In *29th COLING*, pages 1221–1232.

Lazar, Michelle M. 2005. Politicizing gender in discourse: Feminist critical discourse analysis as political perspective and praxis. In Lazar, Michelle M., editor, *Feminist Critical Discourse Analysis: Gender, Power and Ideology in Discourse*, pages 1–28.

Li, Bei, Hui Liu, et al. 2020. Does multi-encoder help? a case study on context-aware neural machine translation. In *58th ACL*, pages 3512–3518.

Lopes, António, M. Amin Farajian, et al. 2020. Document-level neural MT: A systematic comparison. In *22nd EAMT*, pages 225–234.

Papineni, Kishore, Salim Roukos, et al. 2002. BLEU: a Method for Automatic Evaluation of Machine Translation. In *40th ACL*, pages 311–318.

Popović, Maja. 2015. chrF: character n-gram F-score for automatic MT evaluation. In *WMT15*, pages 392–395.

Post, Matt and David Vilar. 2018. Fast lexically constrained decoding with dynamic beam allocation for neural machine translation. In *16th NAACL HLT*, pages 1314–1324.

Prates, Marcelo O. R., Pedro H. Avelar, and Luís C. Lamb. 2020. Assessing gender bias in machine translation: a case study with google translate. *Neural Computing and Applications*, 32(10):6363–6381.

Qin, Ying and Lucia Specia. 2015. Truly exploring multiple references for machine translation evaluation. In *18th EAMT*.

Rei, Ricardo, Craig Stewart, Ana C Farinha, and Alon Lavie. 2020. COMET: A Neural Framework for MT Evaluation. In *EMNLP 2020*, pages 2685–2702.

Saboo, Ashutosh and Timo Baumann. 2019. Integration of dubbing constraints into machine translation. In *WMT19*, pages 94–101.

Saunders, Danielle and Bill Byrne. 2020. Reducing gender bias in neural machine translation as a domain adaptation problem. In *58th ACL*, pages 7724–7736.

Saunders, Danielle, Rosie Sallis, and Bill Byrne. 2022. First the worst: Finding better gender translations during beam search. *Findings of 60th ACL*, pages 3814–3823.

Savoldi, Beatrice, Marco Gaido, et al. 2021. Gender bias in machine translation. *TACL*, 9:845–874.

Savoldi, Beatrice, Marco Gaido, et al. 2022. Under the morphosyntactic lens: A multifaceted evaluation of gender bias in speech translation. In *60th ACL*, pages 1807–1824.

Snover, Matthew, Bonnie Dorr, et al. 2006. A Study of Translation Edit Rate with Targeted Human Annotation. In *7th AMTA*, pages 223–231.

Song, Kai, Yue Zhang, et al. 2019. Code-switching for enhancing NMT with pre-specified translation. In *17th NAACL HLT*, pages 449–459.

Stafanovičs, Artūrs, Mārcis Pinnis, and Toms Bergmanis. 2020. Mitigating Gender Bias in Machine Translation with Target Gender Annotations. In *WMT20*, pages 629–638.

Stahlberg, Dagmar, Friederike Braun, et al. 2007. Representation of the Sexes in Language. *Social communication*, pages 163–187.

Stanovsky, Gabriel, Noah A. Smith, and Luke Zettlemoyer. 2019. Evaluating Gender Bias in Machine Translation. In *57th ACL*, pages 1679–1684.

Sun, Tony, Kellie Webster, et al. 2021. They, Them, Theirs: Rewriting with Gender-Neutral English. *arXiv preprint arXiv:2102.06788*.

van Deemter, Kees. 2009. Utility and language generation: The case of vagueness. *Journal of Philosophical Logic*, 38(6):607–632.

Vanmassenhove, Eva, Christian Hardmeier, and Andy Way. 2018. Getting gender right in neural machine translation. In *EMNLP 2018*, pages 3003–3008.

Vanmassenhove, Eva, Chris Emmery, and Dimitar Shterionov. 2021. NeuTral Rewriter: A rule-based and neural approach to automatic rewriting into gender neutral alternatives. In *EMNLP 2021*, pages 8940–8948.

Wasserman, Benjamin D. and Allyson J. Weseley. 2009. ¿qué? quoi? do languages with grammatical gender promote sexist attitudes? *Sex Roles: A Journal of Research*, 61:634–643.

A Appendix

A.1 Guidelines

The following guidelines for gender-inclusive language were analyzed for this study:

E1 United Nations Economic Commission for Western Asia, 2014
https://archive.unescwa.org/sites/www.unescwa.org/files/page_attachments/1400199_0.pdf.

E2 United Nations, 2018
https://www.un.org/en/gender-inclusive-language/guidelines.shtml.

E3 General Secretariat, Council of the European Union, 2018.
https://www.consilium.europa.eu/media/35446/en_brochure-inclusive-communication-in-the-gsc.pdf

E4 European Parliament, 2018
https://www.europarl.europa.eu/cmsdata/187115/GNL_Guidelines_EN-original.pdf

E5 North Atlantic Treaty Organization, 2020
https://www.nato.int/nato_static_fl2014/assets/pictures/images_mfu/2021/5/pdf/210514-GIL-Manual_en.pdf

E6 Australian Government, 2021
https://www.stylemanual.gov.au/accessible-and-inclusive-content/inclusive-language/gender-and-sexual-diversity

E7 University of Houston, 2022
https://www.uh.edu/marcom/guidelines-policies/inclusive-language/_files/inclusive-language-guide.pdf

E8 Australian National University, n.a.
https://services.anu.edu.au/human-resources/respect-inclusion/gender-inclusive-language

E9 United Nations Women, n.a.
https://authoring.prod.unwomen.org/sites/default/files/Headquarters/Attachments/Sections/Library/Gender-inclusive%20language/Guidelines-on-gender-inclusive-language-en.pdf

E10 University of North Carolina at Chapel Hill, n.a.
https://writingcenter.unc.edu/tips-and-tools/gender-inclusive-language/

E11 University of Pittsburgh, n.a.
https://www.gsws.pitt.edu/resources/faculty-resources/gender-inclusive-non-sexist-language-guidelines-and-resources

E12 Royal Melbourne Institute of Technology, n.a.
https://www.rmit.edu.au/content/dam/rmit/au/en/students/documents/services-support/lgbtiq/guide-inclusive-language.pdf

E13 California State University San Marcos, n.a.
https://www.csusm.edu/ipa/surveys/inclusive-language-guidelines.html

E14 University of Otago, n.a.
https://www.otago.ac.nz/humanresources/working-at-otago/equity/inclusive-language/index.html

E15 The University of Texas at Austin, n.a.
https://intranet.dellmed.utexas.edu/public/inclusive-language-guidelines

I1 Cancelleria Federale Svizzera, 2012
https://www.bk.admin.ch/dam/bk/it/dokumente/sprachdienste/Sprachdienst_it/02/objekt_40366.pdf.download.pdf/guida_al_pari_trattamentolinguisticodidonnaeuomo.pdf

I2 Università di Torino, 2015
https://www.unito.it/sites/default/files/linee_guida_approccio_genere.pdf

I3 Università degli Studi di Padova, 2017
https://www.unipd.it/sites/uni

pd.it/files/2017/Generi%20e%20linguaggi.pdf

I4 Segretariato Generale, Consiglio dell'Unione Europea, 2018
https://www.consilium.europa.eu/it/documents-publications/publications/inclusive-comm-gsc/

I5 Parlamento Europeo, 2018
https://www.europarl.europa.eu/cmsdata/187102/GNL_Guidelines_IT-original.pdf

I6 Università degli Studi di Verona, 2020
https://docs.univr.it/documenti/Documento/allegati/allegati044384.pdf

I7 Università di Bologna, 2020
https://www.unibo.it/it/allegati/linee-guida-per-la-visibilita-del-genere-nella-comunicazione-istituzionale-dell2019universita-di-bologna/@@download/file/Linee-Guida-Genere-2020.pdf

I8 Università degli Studi dell'Aquila, 2020
https://www.univaq.it/include/utilities/blob.php?item=file&table=allegato&id=4925

I9 Università di Siena, 2021
https://www.unisi.it/sites/default/files/allegatiparagrafo/LINEE_GUIDA_Linguaggi_e_Generi.pdf

I10 Istituto Universitario Federale per la Formazione Professionale, 2021
https://www.suffp.swiss/sites/default/files/guida_per_un_linguaggio_inclusivo_20200610.pdf

I11 Università della Calabria, 2021
https://www2.unical.it/portale/strutture/dipartimenti_240/fisica/pariopportunita/Linee%20guida%20Linguaggio%20di%20genere_15%20marzo%2021.pdf

I12 Università degli Studi di Milano, 2021
https://www.unimi.it/sites/default/files/2021-12/Vademecumlinguaggio%20di%20genere_Universit%C3%A0%20degli%20Studi%20di%20Milano.pdf

I13 Università Mediterranea di Reggio Calabria, n.a.
https://www.unirc.it/documentazione/media/files/ateneo/pari_opportunita/File_allegato_2.pdf

I14 Università di Trento, n.a.
https://www.unitn.it/alfresco/download/workspace/SpacesStore/1185b2b5-dcfe-48ef-882b-e7042fe4ff1a/documentolinguaggio29mar%20(1).pdf

I15 Università di Ferrara, n.a.
https://drive.google.com/file/d/1P5Eq2jjoJtTjXGEV7TzyM4XJTcV2PRyp/view

Gender, names and other mysteries: Towards the ambiguous for gender-inclusive translation

Danielle Saunders
Language Weaver
RWS Group
dsaunders@rws.com

Katrina Olsen
Language Weaver
RWS Group
kolsen@rws.com

Abstract

The vast majority of work on gender in MT focuses on 'unambiguous' inputs, where gender markers in the source language are expected to be resolved in the output. Conversely, this paper explores the widespread case where the source sentence lacks explicit gender markers, but the target sentence contains them due to richer grammatical gender. We particularly focus on inputs containing person names.

Investigating such sentence pairs casts a new light on research into MT gender bias and its mitigation. We find that many name-gender co-occurrences in MT data are not resolvable with 'unambiguous gender' in the source language, and that gender-ambiguous examples can make up a large proportion of training examples. From this, we discuss potential steps toward gender-inclusive translation which accepts the ambiguity in both gender and translation.

1 Introduction

Different languages express grammatical gender to differing extents. Where language refers to a person, that person's sociological gender is often expressed via grammatical gender, whether this is simply gendered pronouns in English or profession nouns in German. For machine translation, it is desirable to translate these expressions of gender to the output when they are expressed in the source, and to not express gender in the output which is not implied by the source (Piergentili et al., 2023).

Gender translation is well-defined when translating into a target language that marks gender in the same way as the source language, for the same parts of speech or a subset of them. Difficulties arise when translating into a target language which gender-inflects more parts of speech than the source. This gender translation challenge can be split into two sub-challenges: unambiguous gender translation and ambiguous gender translation. Unambiguous gender translation generally requires gender markers in the source sentence (Renduchintala and Williams, 2022). The challenge is to resolve gendered terms in the target language consistently with the information in the source sentence. For example, translating 'She is an engineer' into German would require that 'engineer' be translated with the feminine form, 'Ingenieurin', not 'Ingenieur'. Most research to date on gender bias and gender handling in NMT has focused on this unambiguous case (Savoldi et al., 2021).

By contrast, the ambiguous case has no gender markers in the source sentence, either surface-level in the form of gendered parts-of-speech or meta-level in the form of speaker tags or user preference. For example, translating 'Taylor is an engineer' into German would still involve choosing a grammatical gender for 'engineer', but it is unclear whether the best option is 'Ingenieur', 'Ingenieurin', or a more inclusive but less commonly used formulation such as 'Ingenieur$*$in'. The goal here is less well-defined. One option is neutralization, avoiding terms implying gender in the output, which may be difficult depending on the output language. Another option, used on a small scale in some commercial systems, is annotating

Eva Vanmassenhove, Beatrive Savoldi, Luisa Bentivogli, Joke Daems & Janiça Hackenbuchner
Proceedings of the 1st Workshop on Gender-Inclusive Translation Technologes, p. 85–93
Tampere, Finland, June 2023.

and producing multiple output translations where source gender is ambiguous (Johnson, 2018). The latter approach, while UI-dependent, has potential for inclusion of new gender-neutral or other non-binary gendered terms.

In this paper, we seek to motivate further research into ambiguous-gender translation. We show that ambiguous-gender translation is an underexplored task relative to its prevalence in corpora. We also perform qualitative exploration of the possibilities and challenges of ambiguous gender translation.

We particularly focus on gender-ambiguous translation with reference to named entities. Predicting gender from person name is unreliable and exclusionary (Section 2.2). However, person names do often co-occur with terms that are gendered in a rich-morphology target language. Sentences containing person names are therefore highly relevant to gender-ambiguous translation.

We first describe related work on gender translation, including some flaws in common treatments of 'unambiguous' gender translation. We then describe and use a simple, high-recall method to identify parallel segments meeting our ambiguous gender criterion, where the model must infer gender despite no reliable markers in the source. We analyse the gender characteristics of the results, focusing on English translation into German, French and Spanish in two domains, OpenSubtitles and Europarl. Finally, we describe some possible directions based on our findings towards gender-inclusive translation technologies, with particular reference to inclusivity of those likely to be misgendered by typical name-gender proxies – anyone whose name does not conform to anglo-centric name-gender associations.

1.1 Related work

Various approaches have been taken to gendering named or otherwise ambiguous entities when gender information is available externally, for example by speaker information. Vanmassenhove et al (2018) incorporate gender information as a tag during training for better translation of first-person sentences. Saunders et al (2022) rerank n-best translations according to grammatical agreement with a known-gender named entity.

Closer to our approach is work by Wang et al (2022), which explores the effect of person names on machine translation absent explicit gender information. They take the position that MT *should* use person names as a proxy for gender where no other gender marker is present, and encourage models to treat names assigned to gender categories similarly. Mota et al (2022) similarly mask all names with the goal of better name translation, and predict gender from names as male, female or unisex in order to maintain grammatical consistency. While we also identify inputs lacking explicit gender markers as a key challenge for MT, we differ by treating names as not having a one-to-one mapping with gender, and propose other ways to determine or control target language gender for sentence pairs with person names.

Měchura (2022) is also close to our work in proposing a taxonomy for gender ambiguities in MT inputs, and a schema for resolving them with respect to a target language; their work focuses on professional nouns, orthogonal to our focus on named entities.

2 Unambiguous gender translation?

In this section, we discuss some assumptions about the resolvability and predictability of gender made in the MT gender literature.

2.1 Pronoun coreference is often ambiguous

Pronouns are often used as gender markers for unambiguous gender. Many machine translation gender test sets including the Gendered Ambiguous Pronoun (GAP) task (Webster et al., 2019) and WinoMT (Stanovsky et al., 2019) involve performing coreference resolution for one pronoun given more than one entity in a sentence.

Currently, most MT systems operate on individual sentences in isolation. However, language within each sentence cannot be known to only refer to entities within the sentence. While GAP allows a 'neither' option for entity resolution, much work in gender translation assumes pronoun coreference is achievable at the sentence-level.

However, pronouns often have multiple plausible antecedents. Even short sentences with a single gendered pronoun and entity (whether person name or profession noun) are not necessarily resolvable. Consider the sentence 'The nurse finished his work', used as a debiasing sentence with unambiguous coreference by Saunders and Byrne (2020). As a hypothetical sentence devoid of context, the nurse can be assumed as unambiguously male, since no other entity was mentioned. However, since utterances are created in context, it is equally valid for this sentence to occur after e.g. 'The technician left early', meaning that the original 'his' coreference is ambiguous.

It is possible to construct truly unambiguous gender-coreferences using, for example, certain types of reflexivization (González et al., 2020; Renduchintala and Williams, 2022) - and the failure of MT on such unambiguous inputs is an important problem. However, entirely unambiguous inputs are not necessarily common. Instead, as we find in Section 4, even sentences with gendered pronouns are frequently ambiguous.

2.2 Person names are not reliably gendered

In the NLP literature, names have frequently been used as a proxy for gender (Ananya et al., 2019; Maudslay et al., 2019). Many given names in an anglo-centric context do have a high correlation with referential gender. However, person names in general do not have a one-to-one mapping with person gender. Some given names are differently gendered in different cultural contexts, e.g. 'Andrea'. Some people, especially non-binary people, choose names to avoid gendered associations, or choose a name that does not correlate with their referential gender (Dev et al., 2021). Many surnames and nicknames are not clearly gendered – and gendered given names are frequently also used as surnames, e.g. 'James'.

Specific named entities may have a known gender, but without additional information, resolving those entities can be difficult. An example is actor Taylor Lautner (he/him), whose wife Taylor (she/her) shares his surname (Lamare, 2022). There may well be further differently gendered Taylor Lautners in the world. Some given names and named entities do have a strong correlation with gender in context: 'Taylor Lautner' in an entertainment-domain sentence written in the 2010s is probably referencing the male actor. However, MT systems do not often have access to information about input domain or time-of-writing. Moreover, even if information about a specific individual's gender is available, it may be ethically undesirable to incorporate this information into the system (Larson, 2017).

Finally, it is undesirable to assume a certain given name will always correspond to a certain gender, in the same way that it is undesirable to assume a vehicle mechanic is male or a nurse female simply because the vast majority are or historically have been. Indeed, the gender associations of given names change with time (Barry and Harper, 1982), a particular challenge for MT where the input lacks time-of-writing context. For all these reasons, offering multiple gendered outputs to the user or having an human-in-the-loop, controllable machine translation with the ability to define and incorporate user preferences may be required for truly gender-inclusive translation.

3 Named entities and ambiguous gender translation

In this section we motivate investigation of named entities for ambiguous gender translation research, and compare named entity recognition (NER) techniques for MT training data.

3.1 Why named entities?

While much work on gender in MT has focused on profession nouns, we concentrate instead on named entities for several reasons: connection to a concrete gender, variety, the relative challenge of detection, and anonymity.

Concreteness: In the ambiguous gender case, profession nouns are often, by convention if not inclusively, translated according to the generic masculine (Silveira, 1980). Named entities by contrast are expected to retain their original gender through any coreferent terms that are gendered in the output. Identifying named entities can therefore be a first step to identifying coreferent words which should be gendered consistently with that entity[1]. This distinction occurs because person names, unlike profession nouns, are likely to have a concrete referent from the perspective of the input sentence's writer. A person name thus has a referential link to a specific person, whether real or fictional, who has some relationship with gender, even if it is unclear to which person the name refers without the author's context (Kripke, 1980).

Variety: Names are a far larger and more diverse category compared to profession nouns. While CareerPlanner[2] lists approximately 12 thousand professions with many near-duplicates, web-

[1]Some prefer a mix of differently gendered referential language (Dev et al., 2021). If language can be produced consistently with one gender, producing consistently with a set of genders is a straightforward extension.

[2]`https://dot-job-descriptions.careerplanner.com`, access Apr 23

site Forebears[3] claims 30 million forenames alone.

Challenge: Detecting person names in natural language presents a different challenge to detecting professional entities. Professional entities are not usually the same in the source and target language and may not be easily distinguishable from other nouns. As a result, identifying professional entities in MT data requires a level of hand curation (Prates et al., 2019). By contrast, person names may often be expected to be identical on both source and target. Exceptions such as transliteration of English names e.g. into Chinese characters (Wan and Verspoor, 1998), or inflection of Slavic named entities (Jacquet et al., 2019), are more complicated, but usually still predictable. However, in our case of translation from English into German, French and Spanish, we make this simplifying assumption.

Anonymity: Finally, there is an increasing interest in anonymity and privacy with respect to NLP models. Models may therefore also be required to translate appropriately when *a* person name is present but the specific person name or gender information is *not* available. Clearly in this situation it is impossible to know if a translation is 'correct' with respect to a specific person's gender—further motivating research and development of systems which expect such ambiguities and handle them gracefully.

3.2 Method

We explore person name detection in parallel data using en-{fr,de,es} bitext from OpenSubtitles (Lison et al., 2018) and Europarl (Koehn, 2005). We preprocess the data by removing all exact duplicate sentence pairs and filtering by length ratio and language id. Table 2 gives line counts after preprocessing.

For our 'title-copy' (TC) approach, we recognize only names containing Unicode characters matching regex `[A-Za-zÀ-ž'-_.]`, beginning with a titlecase character and present in both source and target text. One or more consecutive space-separated tokens can be matched. While a wide variety of possible exceptions exist (McKenzie, 2010), this achieves 100% recall on a list of 200K person names[4].

Additionally, we analyse two techniques using NER with the `en_core_news_sm` model from Spacy 3.2.3[5]. 'Spacy-any' (SA) refers to the subset of TC entities that are also found using the Spacy model NER pipeline on the English source sentence. 'Spacy-person' (SP) refers to the subset of those named entities that Spacy marks as 'person'.

We conduct human evaluation on randomly-selected 100-sentence samples to estimate the precision and false negative rate for each method. For precision we sample from "detected" sentences, marking if the detected entity is interpreted as a person name given sentence context. For false negative we sample 100 "non-detected" sentences and mark if a person name is present. The two annotators are native English speakers with knowledge of the target languages. German is annotated twice with high inter-rater agreement (Cohen's $\kappa = 0.945$); French and Spanish are each annotated once.

3.3 Results: Name detection in parallel data

For the purposes of this paper, we are primarily interested in recall of person names. This is because our ultimate goal is finding target language that may be associated with any person gender. In Table 1 we compare recall in terms of percentage of each dataset retrieved for our three contrastive methods. In terms of recall, we find TC the most effective method, retrieving a far higher percentage of each overall dataset in all cases. However, we do estimate precision and false negative rate, via human evaluation of a 100-sentence random sample for each metric from the matched sentence pairs. False negative rate tracks retrieved percentage of dataset in most cases.

By human evaluation, we determine the precision of the TC method is quite similar to a generic Spacy NER system for all languages and domains. The Spacy-NER system filtered for person identification has significantly higher precision for French and for the Europarl corpora, but a correspondingly high false negative rate. Precision is far lower for TC and SA on Europarl: qualitative analysis suggests this is due to a very high proportion of country and organisation names in the Europarl domain. Even accounting for the lower precision on Europarl, TC recalls a far larger absolute number of person name examples compared to SP, suggesting this is a practical alternative for finding person names in MT data. In the remainder of this paper we exclusively use the TC method when se-

[3]`https://forebears.io/forenames`, access Apr 23

[4]https://github.com/FinNLP/humannames

[5]https://spacy.io

		% Fr	P (↑)	FN (↓)	% De	P (↑)	FN (↓)	% Es	P (↑)	FN (↓)
OS	Title-copy (TC)	42.8	0.81	0.0	13.2	0.80	0.03	18.6	0.75	0.04
	Spacy-any (SA)	30.9	0.83	0.13	9.4	0.78	0.04	11.8	0.91	0.49
	Spacy-person (SP)	19.2	0.96	0.34	5.5	0.75	0.09	7.4	0.97	0.49
EP	Title-copy (TC)	32.7	0.22	0.01	27.0	0.33	0.01	19.3	0.41	0.0
	Spacy-any (SA)	19.6	0.25	0.27	14.5	0.21	0.31	11.1	0.46	0.47
	Spacy-person (SP)	3.6	0.82	0.14	3.7	0.81	0.26	3.7	0.86	0.35

Table 1: Percentage of each dataset marked as containing person names using each method in OpenSubtitles (OS) and Europarl (EP) en-{fr, de, es}. Column P gives estimated precision of name identification based on human evaluation of 100 randomly sampled sentence pairs marked as containing names. Column FN gives false negative rate estimated likewise on a set of 100 pairs marked as not containing names.

		Lines (M)	% N	% P	% N∩P
OS	Fr	3.79	42.8	14.8	6.0
	De	5.85	13.2	11.3	1.6
	Es	48.30	18.6	14.0	2.3
EP	Fr	1.97	32.7	3.6	2.0
	De	1.90	27.0	3.6	2.1
	Es	1.96	19.3	3.6	2.4

Table 2: Line counts for OpenSubtitles (OS) and Europarl (EP) datasets used in this paper after preprocessing, and percentages of each containing N - person names identified by TC - or P - binary English pronouns - or both.

lecting lines containing person-names for analysis.

Given the relative attention in the literature to names versus other gender-associated words such as pronouns, it is interesting to compare their prevalence. In Table 2 we compare the proportion of each dataset containing names – found using the TC method – to the proportion with binary pronouns[6] on the English side. In all cases, more names are found, even accounting for the precisions determined in Table 1. Significantly more segments contain names than pronouns in Europarl and French OpenSubtitles. We also note there is very little overlap between person names and gendered pronouns. Our findings suggest person names are prevalent enough to be their own gender translation challenge.

4 Using named entities to identify target gendered language

In this section we use the best-performing TC person name method from Section 3 to extract lines containing likely person-names, and further analyse their characteristics in terms of gendered language and potential coreference.

4.1 Method

We perform a dependency parse of each target language sentence to identify the head of each person name, and then subsequently any dependents of that head with masculine or feminine grammatical gender. This produces binary gendered terms likely to be associated with a specific named entity. We use this to find likely ambiguous-gender sentences: those with a named entity on the source side and person-referent gendered language on the target (referred to as trg-gendered). We do not attempt to filter for other lexically gendered English terms like 'mother/father', 'fireman/firewoman', etc. We find these terms rare in comparison to names and pronouns.

Note that for our purposes it does not strictly matter whether the named entity is actually coreferent with the gendered terms. This is because we are interested not in translation but in finding co-occurrences that might trigger gender associations in an MT system, correctly or not. However, we do carry out human evaluation to roughly estimate the proportion of cases where target gender is coreferent with the named entity / pronoun to investigate the questions we raise about gender markers in Section 2. The same annotation approach is used as in the previous section, with the question now being whether the gendered target language is plausibly coreferent with the person name. Inter-rater agreement across the task for German is slightly lower than for name marking, but still very high (Cohen's $\kappa = 0.888$);

Given parallel data, we identify named entities as in Section 3. We use the same OpenSubtitles data and Spacy version, for target language parsing use using the relevant {fr,de,es} `core_news_sm` model. As a bonus, we find that filtering for

[6] `grep -Pwi "(she|her|hers|herself|he|him|his|himself)"`. We use a binary match since we find that 'they' is overwhelmingly used in the plural in the OpenSubtitles and Europarl datasets.

		% Fr	Coref	% De	Coref	% Es	Coref
	Trg-gendered TC	27.5	0.42	5.1	0.42	10.9	0.16
OS	- Subset with no src binary pronouns	22.5	0.29	4.2	0.32	9.2	0.20
	- Subset with src binary pronouns	5.0	0.43	0.9	0.65	1.7	0.27
	Trg-gendered TC	30.2	0.16	19.2	0.20	16.9	0.36
EP	- Subset with no src binary pronouns	28.4	0.21	17.7	0.22	15.2	0.29
	- Subset with src binary pronouns	1.8	0.72	1.5	0.77	1.7	0.72

Table 3: Percentages of the original datasets for 'Title-copy' (TC) lines containing target language gendered terms ('trg-gendered'). 'Coref' is estimated coreference proportion – labelled if a person name is coreferent with gendered language in the target – based on human evaluation of 100 randomly sampled matching sentence pairs. Coref scores for the subsets do not necessarily average to the score for the whole set, since evaluation is conducted on independent 100-sentence sample sets.

possibly-coreferent gendered language on the target side seems to result in a higher precision of named entities that are people.

4.2 Results: Names vs pronouns with target language gender

Table 3 gives counts for lines containing person names, with or without binary gendered pronouns in English using the same pronoun match as the previous section, and likely human-referent gendered terms in the target sentence.

Comparing the TC proportions of each dataset in 3 to the trg-gendered TC lines of Table 1, we find that the proportion of lines with likely person names that also contain binary gendered target language in the same subtree as the name in its dependency parse varies significantly based on language and domain. For German and Spanish the proportions of TC lines which also have target gendered language is far lower than French, across both OS and EP domains. This may be because these languages gender fewer parts of speech compared to French.

Source sentences containing likely person names are unlikely to also contain gendered pronouns even when gendered language was also found on the target side. From Table 1 over 80% of sentence pairs containing a likely person name and target gendered language for did not contain a binary gendered source pronoun, making them ambiguous gender inputs. This supports our hypothesis that person-name inputs are a significant and distinct source of person-gender co-occurrences.

4.3 Results: How often are entities coreferent with target gender?

Having found sentences containing likely person names, we are interested in answering two questions:

- How often is a person name associated with grammatically gendered target language?
- How often is a person name actually coreferent with grammatically gendered target language?

The first question is answered by the TC-trg-gendered dataset percentages in Table 3. The second is addressed by the human evaluated coref proportions. We believe there is an important distinction between these points in terms of what an MT system is likely to learn.

We note that a model trained to produce gendered target language words with no grounding in the source sentence may well learn inappropriate triggers and potentially exhibit gender bias in the output. Prior research suggests this is the case for professions via the generic masculine (Tomalin et al., 2021) and for names (Wang et al., 2022). Consider the name 'John', which we find is associated with terms in the grammatical masculine vs feminine in a ratio of 2.2:1 in the EngFra OpenSubtitles data. If a system predominantly associates the name with masculine target language, the name may trigger the grammatical masculine even when coreference does not require it.

While we find that inputs containing person names are frequently associated with gendered language on the target side, actual coreference between names and gendered target language seems rarer. The exception is Europarl sentences containing pronouns, which have a very high proportion of sentences referring to people by both name and title ('president', 'commissioner', etc.)

Consistently fewer than a third of the human evaluated lines without pronouns had the person entity likely coreferent with gendered language on the target side. This is further evidence that using person names as a proxy for inflecting target side

Source	Notes
You let Jax know where she is?	Jax could be told Jax's own location, or someone else's location
What if Kreski's still doing what he did when his brother was alive?	Both 'he' and 'his' in the source could refer to the same or different entities, and neither are necessarily Kreski
You're asking me to kill my son, Ruth.	Ruth could be the listener or son
- That was your father, Finn.	Finn could be the listener or father
They slaughtered my wife, Adalind, and my three children.	Adalind could be the listener, the wife, or a third victim

Table 4: Examples of ambiguous English person-name coreference in the en-de OpenSubtitles samples.

gender may not be fully reliable.

Interestingly, lines with person names and binary pronouns on the source side were evaluated as coreferent at a much higher rate. This seems to be because many sentences containing both names and pronouns were ambiguous. During annotation, two primary sources for English coreferent ambiguity were found. One is, as mentioned previously, the possibility of a pronoun referring to an entity not in the sentence. The other is from two interpretations of comma-inserted names—as an appositive modifying the proceeding noun phrase, such as "Thank God my son, Aethelwulf, is alive." or as a direct address to the listener, such as "Yes, Adam, I'm serious."[7] Examples of both ambiguous cases are given in Table 4.

5 Towards gender-inclusive MT

In this section, we consider what steps towards gender-inclusive MT we might be able to take with access to a wider range of human-referent gendered data. We consider two broad aspects, training and evaluation.

5.1 Training gender inclusive systems

As discussed in related work, prior attempts to keep gender-name consistency in translation have attempted to infer grammatical gender from person name. A more inclusive approach might attempt to infer grammatical gender from target side gender information, and incorporate that information as a tag, as in Vanmassenhove et al (2018) or Saunders et al (2020). Incorporating a tag would let the model learn to associate gender tags with gendered output in the ambiguous case, without requiring either external information or names as a proxy for gender. At inference time, assigning the tag by 'name gender' would be equivalent to approaches in the literature, while a more gender-inclusive approach might produce multiple outputs using different gender tags, or allow tags to be user-controlled.

Tagging training data dependent on the gender of target side sentences has further advantages. First, the source gender tag is related directly to the target grammatical gender. By contrast, leaving a name as a gender proxy assumes a name-gender coreference link which, as found in Table 3, is frequently not present. As a second advantage, the process of tagging these sentence pairs involves directly finding a set of plausibly human-referent gendered language on the target side. These would be a prime target for gender rewriting schemes as described in e.g. Jain et al (2021), potentially including fixed rules to produce neoinflections, but with the bonus of being likely human-referent.

5.2 Evaluating gender inclusive systems

We have demonstrated a high-recall method for obtaining gender-ambiguous sentence pairs with person names in the source and likely human-referent gendered language in the target. We have also shown that we cannot be confident that the human-referent gendered target language is coreferent with the source side entity. This suggests two potential gender translation evaluation schemas.

One would evaluate how translations respond to changing input name. This is similar to the approach explored in Wang et al (2022), but tests for robustness to name stereotyping instead of name-as-gender proxy. An evaluation scheme on these terms would evaluate – and lead the way to addressing – bias affecting those whose names do not exist in an easily predicted 'correct' relationship with their referential gender. The aim of such an evaluation scheme would not be to 'solve' the gender in each context. Instead a system might control

[7] Both examples found in OpenSubtitles en-de

gender in a way related to the *presence* of a person name, but not the actual name.

Another possible scheme would evaluate neutralisation. Our method can identify likely human-referent gendered words in a translation hypothesis. If the goal is to avoid groundless gendered words, an MT system could down-weight hypotheses that contain such words, or an evaluation system score for their presence. While this might not be possible for all target languages, it is increasingly a goal of gender-inclusive translation (Piergentili et al., 2023).

6 Conclusions

This paper proposes a new perspective on gender-inclusive translation technologies. While most research to date has focused on resolving 'unambiguous' gender translation, we discuss the challenges of ambiguous gender translation, where a target language implies gender not grounded in the source. We show that an initial exploration of the ambiguous gender scenario related to named entities suggests possibilities for finding many examples of this scenario in parallel data. We suggest applications for this data both for gender bias mitigation and developing more gender-inclusive systems. Overall, we hope to provide a practical perspective on names, gender, and the inherent ambiguities in gender-inclusive translation.

References

Ananya, Nitya Parthasarthi, and Sameer Singh. 2019. GenderQuant: Quantifying mention-level genderedness. In *Proceedings of the 2019 Conference of the North American Chapter of the Association for Computational Linguistics: Human Language Technologies, Volume 1 (Long and Short Papers)*, pages 2959–2969, Minneapolis, Minnesota, June. Association for Computational Linguistics.

Barry, Herbert and Aylene S Harper. 1982. Evolution of unisex names. *Names*, 30(1):15–22.

Dev, Sunipa, Masoud Monajatipoor, Anaelia Ovalle, Arjun Subramonian, Jeff Phillips, and Kai-Wei Chang. 2021. Harms of gender exclusivity and challenges in non-binary representation in language technologies. In *Proceedings of the 2021 Conference on Empirical Methods in Natural Language Processing*, pages 1968–1994, Online and Punta Cana, Dominican Republic, November. Association for Computational Linguistics.

González, Ana Valeria, Maria Barrett, Rasmus Hvingelby, Kellie Webster, and Anders Søgaard. 2020. Type B reflexivization as an unambiguous testbed for multilingual multi-task gender bias. In *Proceedings of the 2020 Conference on Empirical Methods in Natural Language Processing (EMNLP)*, pages 2637–2648, Online, November. Association for Computational Linguistics.

Jacquet, Guillaume, Jakub Piskorski, Hristo Tanev, and Ralf Steinberger. 2019. JRC TMA-CC: Slavic named entity recognition and linking. participation in the BSNLP-2019 shared task. In *Proceedings of the 7th Workshop on Balto-Slavic Natural Language Processing*, pages 100–104, Florence, Italy, August. Association for Computational Linguistics.

Jain, Nishtha, Maja Popović, Declan Groves, and Eva Vanmassenhove. 2021. Generating gender augmented data for NLP. In *Proceedings of the 3rd Workshop on Gender Bias in Natural Language Processing*, pages 93–102, Online, August. Association for Computational Linguistics.

Johnson, Melvin. 2018. Providing gender-specific translations in Google Translate. (accessed: Aug 2020).

Koehn, Philipp. 2005. Europarl: A parallel corpus for statistical machine translation. In *Proceedings of Machine Translation Summit X: Papers*, pages 79–86, Phuket, Thailand, September 13-15.

Kripke, Saul A. 1980. *Naming and necessity*. Harvard University Press.

Lamare, Amy. 2022. Twilight's Taylor Lautner marries Tay Dome in California wedding. *E News*. (accessed: Apr 2023).

Larson, Brian. 2017. Gender as a variable in natural-language processing: Ethical considerations. In *Proceedings of the First ACL Workshop on Ethics in Natural Language Processing*, pages 1–11, Valencia, Spain, April. Association for Computational Linguistics.

Lison, Pierre, Jörg Tiedemann, and Milen Kouylekov. 2018. OpenSubtitles2018: Statistical rescoring of sentence alignments in large, noisy parallel corpora. In *Proceedings of the Eleventh International Conference on Language Resources and Evaluation (LREC 2018)*, Miyazaki, Japan, May. European Language Resources Association (ELRA).

Maudslay, Rowan Hall, Hila Gonen, Ryan Cotterell, and Simone Teufel. 2019. It's all in the name: Mitigating gender bias with name-based counterfactual data substitution. In *Proceedings of the 2019 Conference on Empirical Methods in Natural Language Processing and the 9th International Joint Conference on Natural Language Processing (EMNLP-IJCNLP)*, pages 5267–5275, Hong Kong, China, November. Association for Computational Linguistics.

McKenzie, Patrick. 2010. Falsehoods programmers believe about names. (accessed: Apr 2023).

Měchura, Michal. 2022. A taxonomy of bias-causing ambiguities in machine translation. In *Proceedings of the 4th Workshop on Gender Bias in Natural Language Processing (GeBNLP)*, pages 168–173, Seattle, Washington, July. Association for Computational Linguistics.

Mota, Pedro, Vera Cabarrão, and Eduardo Farah. 2022. Fast-paced improvements to named entity handling for neural machine translation. In *Proceedings of the 23rd Annual Conference of the European Association for Machine Translation*, pages 141–149, Ghent, Belgium, June. European Association for Machine Translation.

Piergentili, Andrea, Dennis Fucci, Beatrice Savoldi, Luisa Bentivogli, and Matteo Negri. 2023. From inclusive language to gender-neutral machine translation. *arXiv preprint arXiv:2301.10075*.

Prates, Marcelo OR, Pedro H Avelar, and Luís C Lamb. 2019. Assessing gender bias in machine translation: a case study with Google Translate. *Neural Computing and Applications*, pages 1–19.

Renduchintala, Adithya and Adina Williams. 2022. Investigating failures of automatic translation in the case of unambiguous gender. In *Proceedings of the 60th Annual Meeting of the Association for Computational Linguistics (Volume 1: Long Papers)*, pages 3454–3469, Dublin, Ireland, May. Association for Computational Linguistics.

Saunders, Danielle and Bill Byrne. 2020. Reducing gender bias in neural machine translation as a domain adaptation problem. In *Proceedings of the 58th Annual Meeting of the Association for Computational Linguistics*, pages 7724–7736, Online, July. Association for Computational Linguistics.

Saunders, Danielle, Rosie Sallis, and Bill Byrne. 2020. Neural machine translation doesn't translate gender coreference right unless you make it. In *Proceedings of the Second Workshop on Gender Bias in Natural Language Processing*, pages 35–43, Barcelona, Spain (Online), December. Association for Computational Linguistics.

Saunders, Danielle, Rosie Sallis, and Bill Byrne. 2022. First the worst: Finding better gender translations during beam search. In *Findings of the Association for Computational Linguistics: ACL 2022*, pages 3814–3823, Dublin, Ireland, May. Association for Computational Linguistics.

Savoldi, Beatrice, Marco Gaido, Luisa Bentivogli, Matteo Negri, and Marco Turchi. 2021. Gender bias in machine translation. *Transactions of the Association for Computational Linguistics*, 9:845–874.

Silveira, Jeanette. 1980. Generic masculine words and thinking. *Women's Studies International Quarterly*, 3(2-3):165–178.

Stanovsky, Gabriel, Noah A. Smith, and Luke Zettlemoyer. 2019. Evaluating gender bias in machine translation. In *Proceedings of the 57th Annual Meeting of the Association for Computational Linguistics*, pages 1679–1684, Florence, Italy, July. Association for Computational Linguistics.

Tomalin, Marcus, Bill Byrne, Shauna Concannon, D. Saunders, and Stefanie Ullmann. 2021. The Practical Ethics of Bias Reduction in Machine Translation: Why Domain Adaptation is Better than Data Debiasing. *Ethics and Information Technology*, pages 1–15.

Vanmassenhove, Eva, Christian Hardmeier, and Andy Way. 2018. Getting gender right in neural machine translation. In *Proceedings of the 2018 Conference on Empirical Methods in Natural Language Processing*, pages 3003–3008, Brussels, Belgium, October-November. Association for Computational Linguistics.

Wan, Stephen and Cornelia Maria Verspoor. 1998. Automatic English-Chinese name transliteration for development of multilingual resources. In *36th Annual Meeting of the Association for Computational Linguistics and 17th International Conference on Computational Linguistics, Volume 2*, pages 1352–1356, Montreal, Quebec, Canada, August. Association for Computational Linguistics.

Wang, Jun, Benjamin Rubinstein, and Trevor Cohn. 2022. Measuring and mitigating name biases in neural machine translation. In *Proceedings of the 60th Annual Meeting of the Association for Computational Linguistics (Volume 1: Long Papers)*, pages 2576–2590, Dublin, Ireland, May. Association for Computational Linguistics.

Webster, Kellie, Marta R. Costa-jussà, Christian Hardmeier, and Will Radford. 2019. Gendered ambiguous pronoun (GAP) shared task at the gender bias in NLP workshop 2019. In *Proceedings of the First Workshop on Gender Bias in Natural Language Processing*, pages 1–7, Florence, Italy, August. Association for Computational Linguistics.

How adaptive is adaptive machine translation, really? A gender-neutral language use case

Aida Kostikova
Ghent University
aida.kostikova@ugent.be

Joke Daems
Ghent University
joke.daems@ugent.be

Todor Lazarov
New Bulgarian University
tdlazarov@gmail.com

Abstract

This study examines the effectiveness of adaptive machine translation (AMT) for gender-neutral language (GNL) use in English-German translation using the ModernMT engine. It investigates gender bias in initial output and adaptability to two distinct GNL strategies, as well as the influence of translation memory (TM) use on adaptivity. Findings indicate that despite inherent gender bias, machine translation (MT) systems show potential for adapting to GNL with appropriate exposure and training, highlighting the importance of customisation, exposure to diverse examples, and better representation of different forms for enhancing gender-fair translation strategies.

1 Introduction

With increasing adoption of GNL, its reflection in natural language processing (NLP) applications like MT becomes vital. Ignoring GNL trends can perpetuate biased representations and inequalities (Savoldi et al., 2021), and also much of prior work in the field of gender bias is built on techniques which assume gender is binary. AMT, which learns from users and adjusts to personal linguistic preferences (Bentivogli et al., 2015), may offer promise for ensuring GNL use in MT, especially given the fact that it reduces post-editing efforts and has shown certain potential for empowering the human in the loop (Martikainen, 2022).

This study evaluates the effectiveness of AMT for GNL use, focusing on non-binary language in English-German translation using the ModernMT[1] engine. Our research, while somewhat aligned with the works of Saunders et al. (2020), Sun et al. (2021) and Vanmassenhove et al. (2021) in their intent to address gender neutrality in MT, offers a distinct approach. While Sun et al. and Vanmassenhove et al. advocate for post-processing steps to rewrite gendered sentences into gender-neutral ones using either rule-based or neural approaches, and Saunders et al. fine-tune a base model with synthetic datasets, our research investigates the real-time adaptability of AMT systems to naturally integrate GNL into its translations. Their approaches, although effective, often require access to and control over the internal mechanisms of the MT system or extensive task-specific datasets, which is not always feasible with black-box systems like ModernMT. Our study, on the other hand, explores how these black-box systems can dynamically adapt to GNL in their translation process without the need for post-processing steps or specialised fine-tuning. In this way, we assess the system's intrinsic ability to adjust to GNL, offering a more dynamic and contextual view of how these systems may cope with evolving language trends over the long run.

We examine two distinct GNL strategies, such as gender asterisk and De-E-System. The gender asterisk form, which is increasingly utilised in German to inclusively represent all genders, is constructed by appending an asterisk before the gender-specific suffix (e.g., *Ärzt*innen*). Conversely, the De-E-System, which was developed by the Association for Gender Neutral German (Verein für geschlechtsneutrales Deutsch[2]) employs the concept of "Inklusivum", a proposed fourth grammatical gender. This system introduces new declination rules and modifications for forming gender-neutral articles, nouns, and pronouns: for example, in this system, nouns typically end with either *-e* or *-re*, accompanied by the gender-neutral article *de*: *de Schülere (student), de Autore (author).*

Two versions of ModernMT were deployed in this study: a system without the use of TM, as well as its customised variant, which was exposed to a TM containing gender-neutral forms. The research investigates whether AMT exhibits gender bias in initial output, analyses its adaptability when working with two conceptually different GNL strategies, the role of TM in improving results, as well as factors influencing engine adaptation success.

[1] https://www.modernmt.com/

[2] https://geschlechtsneutral.net/gesamtsystem/

Eva Vanmassenhove, Beatrive Savoldi, Luisa Bentivogli, Joke Daems & Janiça Hackenbuchner
Proceedings of the 1st Workshop on Gender-Inclusive Translation Technologes, p. 95–97
Tampere, Finland, June 2023.

2 Data and Methodology

Four scenarios were studied: using gender asterisk and De-E-System, each with and without TM, using texts based on the 2006 Court Procedures Rules for the Australian Capital Territory, which have been selected due to the fact that they inherently follow GNL principles in English. However, they also contain numerous elements — specifically, terms denoting professional roles or titles (as *administrator, real estate agent, director of public prosecutions*) — which do not hold gendered connotations in English but could potentially introduce gender bias when translated into German. The study includes 15 sentences for each of the 15 selected role-related nouns that could require gender-neutral adaptation during translation. For instance, consider the sentence: *The real estate agent might be appointed to market the land and conduct the sale*. In German, this could be translated using the gender asterisk as *Die*der Immobilienmakler*in könnte beauftragt werden, das Grundstück zu vermarkten und den Verkauf durchzuführen*, or with the De-E-System as *De Immobilienmaklere könnte beauftragt werden, das Grundstück zu vermarkten und den Verkauf durchzuführen*.

The evaluation of the engine's adaptive performance was conducted through a blend of quantitative and qualitative methods. For a quantitative perspective, we utilized two automatic metrics, character-based translation edit rate (CharacTER) and keystrokes ratio (KSR), and we computed the total number of adapted segments. While these metrics do not directly measure gender bias or adaptivity rate, they provide essential insights into the editing effort required to correct the engine's output, thus serving as proxies for its adaptive performance, as lower values for CharacTER and KSR would suggest that the engine is adapting well to the GNL. These metrics also enable a comparison of results across different experiments, such as those employing various GNL strategies or comparing performance with and without TM utilisation.

For a more nuanced and targeted understanding of gender bias in the translation process, we complemented these metrics with a qualitative content analysis of specific instances of adaptation and a close examination of gender bias in the initial output.

3 Results

3.1 Gender bias in the adaptive MT output

Our findings align with previous research in the field of gender bias in MT (Monti, 2020; Savoldi et al., 2021), indicating that ModernMT also exhibits gender bias in their output when using both gender-neutral strategies. Analysis showed significant masculine bias in both experiments, with De-E-System having higher bias with TM (87% and 88% masculine translations in untrained and trained engines, respectively; presence of gender-neutral forms increased by 2.7%). Conversely, gender asterisk strategy exhibited less bias: without TM, 78% segments were masculine; with TM, masculine translations dropped by 17.2% and gender-neutral translations increased by 22.7%. It should be noted that these percentages represent an absolute increase in gender-neutral translations. By focusing on absolute changes, we could directly observe the shifts in translation behaviour due to the integration of the TM with gender-neutral forms, thus offering a clearer understanding of the potential of AMT for adopting GNL strategies.

Interestingly, some nouns were consistently translated with feminine gender, and all such instances were related to specific roles, such as *appellant, defendant* and *plaintiff*, who are less likely to be involved in decision-making, managing, and investigating functions (as opposed to, for instance, *employer, examiner, expert, liquidator*, which were predominantly translated with masculine gender). This discrepancy potentially indicates two sources of bias: pre-existing and technical bias (Friedman and Nissenbaum, 1996).

Pre-existing bias refers precisely to any asymmetries which are rooted in society at large or which reflect personal biases of individuals responsible for the system development. Technical bias, in contrast, manifests in the stages of data collection, system design, training, and testing procedures for MT models. In the context of our research, the fact that some roles were predominantly assigned masculine translations, while others consistently appeared with feminine connotations, might indicate such deep-rooted pre-existing biases within the training data. Moreover, according to the study of European Commission for the Efficiency of Justice (CEPEJ, 2016), although women frequently succeed in entering the legal field, their progression into senior positions tends to be slower. Thus, the achieved result might be explained by asymmetries present in the data used by the MT system.

3.2 Overall adaptivity to GNL

The percentage of gender-neutral translations for the experiments demonstrate diverse adaptability of ModernMT when handling GNL. And although the overall adaptation rate remains relatively low, along with inconsistent adaptation across all four experiments in this study, some clear trends were observed.

Firstly, the engine demonstrated better adaptation over time when working with the gender asterisk system, with an increased number of adapted segments towards the end of the project (by the last two or three words) for both untrained and trained engines. Secondly, it was determined that, to achieve such progress, it is essential for the system to have sufficient exposure to gender-neutral words in various forms. This includes considering grammatical number, case, and different types of articles, as for instance, the system struggled with adapting to plurals due to an insufficient number of examples in the corpus. This highlights the importance of ensuring the variability and exposure to different grammatical and syntactical structures, possibly with the help of TM.

This discrepancy in the adaptation success of the gender asterisk method over the De-E-System could be attributed to a combination of factors. First, the wider prevalence of gender asterisk forms in the German language (Burtscher et al., 2022) may inherently favour this method, as its similarity to conventional language forms likely aids model recognition. Second, the instance-based learning approach of ModernMT (Piergentili et al., 2023) can help the system to learn from similar, even non-identical instances, and generalise to unseen examples. This ability, when coupled with the potential presence of gender-neutral structures resembling the gender asterisk method in ModernMT's training data, could have facilitated the engine's capacity to adapt more effectively to this method. These contributing factors provide a plausible explanation for the observed discrepancy, wherein the model displayed a superior adaptation to the gender asterisk approach as compared to the De-E-System.

4 Conclusion and Future Research

These findings suggest that AMT systems, despite being prone to gender bias, have the potential to adapt to GNL forms (especially if they are more widespread) with appropriate exposure, although further refinement and optimisation are necessary to improve their adaptability to GNL. TMs facilitated adaptation by exposing the system to diverse GNL examples, thus enhancing its recognition and adaptation of gender-neutral variants. Solutions for better customisation (Lardelli and Gromann, 2023) ensuring better representation of different forms for various strategies will be crucial in advancing gender-fair translation strategies.

It is important to acknowledge that the limited number of sentences may not fully capture all the nuances of translating GNL in broader contexts. This study, therefore, should be considered a preliminary exploration of this complex linguistic area. Future research is necessary to validate these results in more extensive and diverse corpora, which would provide a more comprehensive understanding of AMT systems' performance when dealing with GNL.

References

Burtscher, S., Spiel, K., Klausner, L.D., Lardelli, M. and Gromann, D. 2022. "Es geht um Respekt, nicht um Technologie": Erkenntnisse aus einem Interessensgruppen-übergreifenden Workshop zu genderfairer Sprache und Sprachtechnologie. *Proceedings of Mensch und Computer 2022 (pp. 106-118).*

Bentivogli, L., Bertoldi, N., Cettolo, M., Federico, M., Negri, M. and Turchi, M. 2015. On the evaluation of adaptive machine translation for human post-editing. *IEEE/ACM Transactions on Audio, Speech, and Language Processing*, 24(2), pp.388-399.

CEPEJ Report, European Commission for the Efficiency of Justice. (2016). *Evaluation of European judicial systems - CEPEJ report.*

Friedman, B., and Nissenbaum, H. (1996). Bias in computer systems. In *ACM Transactions on Information Systems (TOIS), 14(3)*, pp. 330–347.

Lardelli, M. and Gromann, D. 2022. Gender-Fair (Machine) Translation. *New Trends in Translation and Technology 2022*, p.166.

Martikainen, H. 2022. *Ghosts in the machine: Can adaptive MT help reclaim a place for the human in the loop?*

Monti, J. 2020. Gender issues in machine translation: An unsolved problem? *The Routledge Handbook of Translation, Feminism and Gender*, pp. 457-468.

Savoldi, B., Gaido, M., Bentivogli, L., Negri, M., Turchi, M. 2021. Gender Bias in Machine Translation. Transactions of the Association for Computational Linguistics; 9, pp. 845–874.

Saunders, D., Sallis, R., and Byrne, B. (2020). Neural machine translation doesn't translate gender coreference right unless you make it. *Proceedings of the Second Workshop on Gender Bias in Natural Language Processing*, pp. 35–43.

Sun, T., Webster, K., Shah, A., Wang, W.Y. and Johnson, M. (2021) They, them, theirs: Rewriting with gender-neutral English. *arXiv preprint arXiv:2102.06788.*

Piergentili, A., Fucci, D., Savoldi, B., Bentivogli, L. and Negri, M. 2023. From Inclusive Language to Gender-Neutral Machine Translation. *arXiv preprint arXiv:2301.10075.*

Vanmassenhove, E., Emmery, C. and Shterionov, D. (2021). NeuTral Rewriter: A Rule-Based and Neural Approach to Automatic Rewriting into Gender-Neutral Alternatives. *arXiv preprint arXiv:2109.06105.*

Association for Computational Linguistics
209 N. Eighth Street
Stroudsburg, Pennsylvania 18360

ISBN 978-1-7138-8996-0

CURRAN ASSOCIATES INC.
proceedings.com